H. AVERC

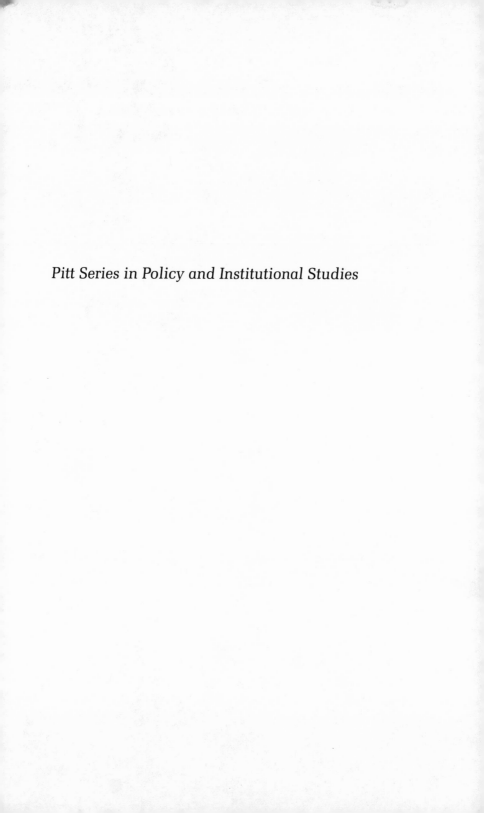

Pitt Series in Policy and Institutional Studies

Private Markets and Public Intervention

A Primer for Policy Designers

HARVEY AVERCH

University of Pittsburgh Press

Published by the University of Pittsburgh Press, Pittsburgh, Pa.
15260
Published in the United Kingdom by BT Press
17 Avenue Mansions, Finchley Road, London NW3 7AX
Copyright © 1990, University of Pittsburgh Press
All rights reserved
Baker & Taylor International, London
Manufactured in the United States of America

Library of Congress Cataloging-in-Publication Data

Averch, Harvey A.
  Private markets and public intervention : a primer for policy
designers, c 1990.
      p. cm.—(Pitt series in policy and institutional studies)
    Includes bibliographical references.
    ISBN 0-8229-3647-X.—ISBN 0-8229-5437-0 (pbk.)
    1. Policy sciences—Cost effectiveness.   2. Bureaucracy—
United States—Cost effectiveness.   3. Trade regulation—United
States—Cost effectiveness.   4. Deregulation—United States—
Cost effectiveness.   5. Privatization—United States—Cost
effectiveness. I. Title. II. Series.
H97.A77   1990
338.973—
dc20   90-30612
                                                            CIP

To the memory of my parents,
Gussie and Louis Averch

Contents

Preface

Today many Americans believe that firms and markets can and will deliver public services more efficiently than bureaus, so politicians try to transfer public services to the private sector. Certainly, deregulation and privatization are popular solutions for economic and social problems in the early 1990s. Yesterday Americans believed that private markets would never adequately account for environmental, health, and safety costs incurred in production. As a result, extensive environmental, health, and safety regulation forced firms to consider such costs. But then Americans discovered that social regulation dampened incentives to innovate, so politicians and administrators began searching for ways to temper negative impacts on private incentives. They came up with new demands and procedures for central review, thus regulating the regulators.

No doubt the future holds more shifts in perceptions of what works and what fails. Past shifts, it seemed to me while in federal service, derived more from current intellectual fashions and changing political winds than they did from newly discovered facts or significantly improved theory.

Faced with competing claims about markets and government, I found that neither politicians nor high-level bureaucrats understood the alternatives for resource allocation available to them. I had long tried to find primers that would give my staff, my superiors, and me simple and compact accounts of how these strategies worked. Discussions in economics texts of the relative problem-solving merits of markets, bureaus, or regulation were both casual and narrow. The texts did not exhibit much sophistication about the politically constrained decision making that goes on—and must go on—in all bureaus. Their discussions of bureaucratic behavior, if provided at all, usually came after more or less rigorous proofs of the efficiency of competitive markets. They showed how market failure might occasionally require action or intervention by government agencies. But they provided little analysis of whether or when such intervention would be feasible or effective.

Surprisingly, for a discipline that believed in the pursuit of constrained self-interest, economics texts assumed that public agencies were truly interested in curing failure. Indeed, from the perspective of economics, cure or correction was the primary reason bureaus existed at all. Once economic analysis revealed a market failure, there was never any difficulty carrying out the appropriate corrections. Bureaus, by implication, could always design and run cost-effective programs relative to a well-identified failure. However, the texts presented no tools or methods that would induce bureaus to adopt programs or policies that would be socially cost-effective. They left this as an unsolved political science or policy science problem.

In contrast, policy analysis texts were very long on technical methods and algorithms derived from economics, operations research, and management science. Agency heads truly in command of their organizations might use these to optimize resource allocation relative to their objectives. But policy analysis as exhibited in the texts provided little guidance on how to design and sustain workable organizations that operated under political constraints, guidance, and incentives. The politics of policy making was left to a somewhat underdeveloped science of organization and implementation.

As a professor of economics, policy science, and public administration, I found that my students could eventually manipulate the graphs and mathematics of formal microeconomics and could learn to make standard benefit-cost calculations. However, they had little sense of how or why market systems work, their public prerequisites, how to know when markets were failing, what to do when they did fail, or whether failure mattered in any significant way other than as some invisible loss in overall efficiency.

My students certainly had no idea of when and why bureaucratic supply of goods and services or public regulation might be reasonable substitutes for the free market. Worst of all, their ability to untangle claims about the superiority of one over another was very weak. Yet I knew that when they became practicing economists or analysts, at some time in their careers, they would be engaged in clarifying, judging, and refuting claims about the virtues and vices of markets, bureaus, or regulation. And I knew the claims would go far beyond relative capabilities in allocating resources efficiently in a static environment.

My experience with American students was reinforced by a teaching assignment in China in the summer of 1985. My students at the Dalian Institute of Technology in northeast China were middle-level industrial managers from every province. I taught them research and development (R&D) policy and management in the context of firms and markets. But the very concept of private markets and firms as devices for the efficient allocation of resources was very hard for them to grasp. They had even greater difficulty understanding that decision makers might have a choice between public and private technologies and institutions for allocating resources. My Chinese students did have access to standard American texts on managerial economics, but these did not contain any comparative discussions of alternatives in capitalist economies, let alone socialist ones.

As a result, then, of my government service and teaching experience, in this book I try to set out the virtues and defects of common public strategies for delivering resources or for guiding and motivating others to deliver them. I discuss the major substantive strategies for attacking and solving public problems—markets, bureaus, regulation, ex ante planning and budgeting, ex post evaluation, and two process strategies: cost-benefit analysis, and systems analysis. I have always believed that understanding any of these requires some historical background on how and why they came into use, and therefore each discussion of a strategy begins with a historical sketch.

So far, the policy analysis craft has advanced by discovering failures and pitfalls and by heralding negative findings— what does not work. Presumably, decision making that is sensitive to potential failures and pitfalls and accounts for them becomes improved decision making. Each discussion of a particular strategy therefore contains a list of generic failures or pitfalls—that is, the ones that are *inherent* in using the strategy even when it is well designed and executed. They must be faced consciously. There is no quick fix for them. More competent administrators, less red tape, or reorganization will not necessarily help. The propensity to fail means not that strategies always fail but that, when they do, it will be along characteristic lines and that decision makers should be aware of these lines in choosing among strategies.

Chapter 11 discusses what we know about performance across different strategies.

Besides public officials, the book is also targeted for upper-division and first-year graduate students in policy analysis and public administration. The only economics background I assume on the part of readers is prior or concurrent exposure to a basic microeconomics course. The only mathematical background I assume is modest familiarity with constrained optimization. This should not be a serious barrier, because many policy analysis and public administration programs cover optimization early. Students in microeconomics might also find some of the discussion useful. Texts in microeconomic theory usually provide little discussion of the propensity to innovate in markets or bureaus, even though innovation, the creation of new products and processes, may be far more important for social welfare than achieving efficiency using fixed products and processes.

The notes contain additional comments and references so that readers may check and verify discussion in the main text and go beyond it if they wish. Furthermore, the bibliography contains comments on many sources cited in the notes. These comments indicate only what I believe is most worthy in them for the purposes at hand, not their worth for every purpose.

I wrote early draft chapters of this book in 1984–85 while I was on leave from the National Science Foundation and serving as visiting professor of policy science and economics at the University of Maryland, Baltimore County. I thank the foundation and the university for providing the time to review a very diverse literature. I also thank Len Lederman of the foundation for the thoughtful and careful reading he gave each chapter, even though I always gave him short turnaround time. Eileen Collins, also of the foundation, provided highly perceptive criticism at a crucial stage in the planning of the book.

I completed the final draft at Florida International University where I am now professor of public administration. I thank my colleague Howard Frank for timely comments from a public administration perspective. Thanks go also to Amy Stanley, of FIU's North Campus Computer Services, for care and diligence in word processing the final version of the manuscript.

**Private Markets
and Public
Intervention**

Chapter 1
Introduction

THIS BOOK is concerned with the description, analysis, and appraisal of common strategies for solving problems in public policy. It presents the logic behind strategies commonly met in public debate in the United States. It provides some criteria and questions for use in thinking about putting alternatives into practice, changing them, or abolishing them. The actual choice of any strategy depends mainly on history and politics. To the extent that any choice is rational, broad social, economic, and political comparisons are necessary. From a decision maker's perspective, some strategies are efficient but not fast; some may work fast but may be inefficient and waste resources; some are corrigible in the face of suddenly discovered or revealed error, and some are not. Some can acquire political support and some cannot. Given differences in expected performance, a generic problem for decision makers is making an informed, balanced, comprehensive judgment or appraisal of relative merit.[1]

Now, government agencies all have internal logics for preferring one strategy over another. In the federal government, practically all agencies want more budget and staff,[2] traditional signs of success and the approval of sponsors, and which in turn increase agencies' power to gain future resources. For example, regulators conceivably may be able to acquire more resources by central control and directives than by creating markets to distribute pollution rights. The acquisition of additional budget or staff, however, is not a reason they can offer publicly, salient as it may be internally. Agencies must have some publicly defensible and persuasive reasons for preferring the strategies they will design, operate, and control centrally.[3] Abating pollution by creating and operating new markets may take too long. The long-run efficiency produced by a market that is working well may offend strongly held notions of political equity and equal sharing. Getting any pollution control at all may require trading some efficiency for a little more equity—for example, setting minimal standards that all polluters have to meet—even though total resources invested in pollution control are greater than they need be.

This book, then, deals with the substantive, public reasons or justifications for choosing one strategy over another. Examples of such reasons are: effectiveness, efficiency, expected speed in problem solving, susceptibility to failure or breakdown, and the direct or indirect impacts of one strategy on the performance of some other of high value. Regulation that forces firms to use the best available technology for reducing pollution may well succeed. However, they may reduce market incentives to innovate, since firms may end up concentrating on "defensive" R&D to achieve minimal compliance. Hence decision makers have to weigh the likelihood of spillovers or indirect impacts as well as the direct impacts. They have to find reasonable political and economic trade-offs.

AN ILLUSTRATIVE DEBATE OVER STRATEGIES: MARKETS, BUREAUS, AND INNOVATION

Over the last thirty years there has been intense debate about whether the federal government needs to define and administer a formal policy on industrial innovation. The basic issue here concerns the innovation-inducing virtues of market-based strategies versus those that are centrally designed and executed.[4] Depending on the particular advocate, innovation policy is supposed to help in maintaining international economic competitiveness, in revitalizing failing industries, in encouraging new industries, or in encouraging a socially "appropriate" or "meritorious" flow of new goods and services.

Facts play some role in this debate. For instance, advocates cite the declining rate of patent filings in the United

States by U.S. firms and the increasing rate of filings by foreign firms as evidence that the United States is losing its innovative powers.[5] Characteristics and facts without strong theory leaves room for alternate interpretations. Thus declining patenting may signal a shift to other means of pursuing rights or even rapid technological change. However, much of the debate has concerned assertions and beliefs about the relative merits of markets in maintaining a dynamic economy compared to government programs or guidance.

Opponents of central innovation policy offer two principal arguments against it: first, it would be ineffective; and second, if the government did enforce a policy and it turned out to be effective, it would make things worse, sending the wrong signals to the private sector. It would make the climate for innovation more uncertain and would destroy the flexibility any open economy needs to respond to changing domestic and world markets.

Those who prefer centrally directed policies or programs for innovation justify them on grounds of clearly perceived national needs. Either markets cannot satisfy these needs, or they do not do so fast enough. In contrast, these advocates see bureaus as able to cope and to do so quickly. They believe bureaus know more, collectively, than anyone in the private sector and that they will act effectively on the basis of their superior knowledge.

Advocates of market solutions and private incentives argue that technological innovation has positive social outcomes if, and only if, some market process confirms it. This means that consumers are willing to pay for the innovation and producers are willing to supply it at somewhere near its social opportunity cost. If we allow markets to work, they will find innovations that meet appropriate economic tests. Thus market advocates argue that public policy interventions ought to be limited to well-identified and socially significant cases of market failure and to the delivery of certain public goods. But they identify very few cases of market failure that deserve correction and only a few goods, like national defense, that really require public delivery.[6]

To market advocates, engaging or increasing private incentives always gives better results than any bureaucratic programs or guidance. In fact, they believe pervasive federal programs, particularly regulation, are themselves one of the greatest threats to innovation. Regulation causes distortions in the market's technological perceptions. Thus we have to make certain that federal activity, at most, is limited to providing or supporting "generic" information for all industries and to correcting the few market failures that cannot be cured by changing private incentives or by creating new markets. The best thing that the federal government can do for innovation, in such a view, is to remove its own regulatory presence from the marketplace. Deregulation is automatically good innovation policy.

Even if bureaus and markets just happened to have the same information, the latter have safeguards against error that public agencies cannot ever have. Public agencies cannot tolerate competing interpretations of technological and economic information, so there is no hedge against adopting erroneous innovations. Markets, however, contain many actors dedicated to exploring potential innovations; if some guess wrong, others will guess right. Hence markets are unlikely to overlook beneficial technologies (high private and social rates of return). Conversely, markets will not pursue for very long innovations that provide insufficient private returns. In contrast, government has the resources to pursue innovations long after low social returns have become highly visible. Indeed, political and bureaucratic factors exist that almost guarantee such a pursuit.[7]

The striking thing about this debate is how little certain knowledge we have about its core. People who like competitive market systems argue the superiority of markets over government agencies in sizing up new technological opportunities. At a deeper level, they argue that local, specific knowledge held in markets is more important than aggregate, cross-market knowledge held by bureaus and that the market employs its information in superior ways.

However, proving such contentions is far more difficult than proving the ability of markets to allocate fixed resources more efficiently.[8]

THE ANALYTICAL TASK

Analysts can do some thing to improve the quality of argument in political economy. They can be as explicit as possible about the properties of the strategies being proposed by contending parties. They can estimate how each competing alternative would work out if decision makers selected it. Finally, they can be on the lookout for the failure of strategies and can design programs to minimize social damage when failure occurs.

Thinking hard about failure is important in at least two different ways. First, if decision makers and the public agree on the merits of solving a social problem, they would not want to choose programs or activities that prevent solution or, even worse, aggravate the original problem.[9] Second, failures are strong political and organizational signals; they are far more important than successes, politically and bureaucratically. Failure is visible and costly.[10] Consequently, sensitizing decision makers to ask their advisers and constituents about failure is an important policy analysis job. It is frequently neglected.

AIM AND DESIGN OF THE BOOK

This book describes how common strategies work and the general or structural reasons why they may fail, and it makes appraisals of each. The seven are: markets, bureaus, regulation, planning and budgeting, benefit-cost, systems analysis, and evaluation. Chapter 2 defines a set of appraisal factors—political, economic, and organizational—applied to these strategies. For each strategy there is a discussion of (1) the historical development; (2) a description of how the strategy would work ideally; (3) an explanation of the necessary or sufficient conditions that permit it to work; (4) a list of potential failures; and (5) a judgment or appraisal.

Chapter 11 compares strategies. It argues that there is no dominant one when we are concerned with multiple criteria of performance. This chapter also presents more support for the testing and appraisal function.

Chapter 2
Appraisal of Strategies

ALTHOUGH THERE ARE no generally agreed-upon criteria for deciding between diverse strategies, actual practice is important as a guide in selecting questions or criteria.[1] If we examine a large number of debates over appropriate strategies, and if decision makers and practicing policy designers pose the same questions over and over again, then we should take them seriously. For example, if decision makers frequently ask their advisers about timeliness or political acceptability when confronting alternatives, then it is reasonable to include them in ex ante analysis and advice.[2]

TEN REASONABLE CRITERIA

This chapter uses ten criteria or factors in appraising alternative strategies: (1) static efficiency, (2) dynamic efficiency, (3) "invisibility," (4) robustness, (5) timeliness, (6) stakeholder equity, (7) corrigibility, (8) public acceptability, (9) simplicity, and (10) cost. I have constructed this list to combine concerns about the efficient use of resources at one point in time and over time; political and organizational concerns involved in getting things done in bureaus, at least in the United States; and the concerns of decision makers in gaining credit for policies and programs that work and avoiding blame for those that do not. Public policy and real world allocation of resources cannot be based on high performance on some single criterion. Economists, for example, who always value efficiency very highly, have to contend with competitors who value political feasibility highly or palatability to the electorate.

8

These are not the only factors that might be of concern, and we could certainly construct a longer list. Again, if we look to actual practice, choices between policy alternatives usually turn on a few coarse-grained criteria rather than many fine-grained ones. If some strategy rates comparatively well on most of the ten proposed here, then we can say that adoption seems warranted. There may be more than one warranted strategy. Where, on the basis of available information, one strategy is as good as another, decision makers can simply choose from those with strong warrants. They may, of course, always elect to wait for more information before deciding anything, or they may adopt experimental strategies that produce much more precise information before action is taken. However, waiting has social and bureaucratic costs, too.[3] Getting a problem solved in a reasonable time must be part of any appraisal.

Decision makers can also try to apply higher-order criteria to those strategies that seem to be justified. But expending time and resources on ex ante, higher-order inquiry often has diminishing returns. Some potentially effective strategies may have only a small window of opportunity to get started. Very prolonged decision time increases production and transactions costs and reduces the total number of strategies.[4] If, ex ante, decision makers design and select corrigible strategies, then, ex post, they should be able to evaluate actual outcomes and make marginal adjustments, or they may be able to shift strategies.

RELATIVE WEIGHTS

The weights that decision makers and designers assign to appraisal criteria are often different from those suggested by standard definitions of rational, optimizing behavior. The first three criteria, for example, derive from fundamental notions in microeconomic theory about the most appropriate use of inputs.[5] Theory and rhetoric strongly suggest that efficient use of resources should be given heavy weight in any decision. However, decision makers have little patience with considerations of efficiency, and these are never given as much weight in actual decisions as economists believe they should have.

In contrast, timeliness is highly important to decision makers, but less so or not at all in economics. The short run and the long run in economic theory refer not to any real amounts of time, but time in which one has limited flexibility in making decisions and time in which one has great freedom to make decisions. However, people with a strong preference for market strategies believe that they will be fast in real time as well as efficient.[6]

Strategies that work fast but waste resources are not considered of much value in economics. However, waste of resources is much more tolerable to decision makers and bureaus than time lost. To a decision maker considering the use of markets to solve social problems, timeliness may be critical—if only because solutions that occur within the expected tenure of the decision maker must be preferable to those that do not. In the United States high-level decision makers arrive in office with an agenda they have promised to implement during their tenure, but their actual tenure is usually short.

In sum, the design of public policy involves balancing multiple objectives and criteria. Paradoxically, single-minded pursuit of efficiency, neglecting other objectives, may well result in greater inefficiency. Bureaus that pursue only efficiency, for example, may encounter constituents' claims for more equity, and the constituents may have a strong political voice with sponsors. Thus decision makers may well reject policies or programs that rank high on the efficient use of resources and accept relatively inefficient ones that rank high on other important objectives.

STATIC EFFICIENCY

At any given time any organization has fixed resources and production technologies. Since these are costly to acquire and can be deployed in alternate ways, then, at minimum, they should not be wasted. They should be used efficiently. Static efficiency means that an organization produces as much of a good or service as it can with its fixed resources and technology, without decreasing the output of other goods or services that it could produce using the same resources and technologies.[7] In other words, an organization is productively efficient when there exists no combination of goods and services such that it can produce more of one without having to reduce the production of another.[8]

THE CASE OF THE FIRM

Suppose a firm has fixed amounts of resources and unchanging production technologies and makes just two goods. Then it has a production possibility frontier, *AB* in figure 1, that is technologically determined. *AB* shows all the combinations of *A* and *B* that are technologically feasible. The slope of the production possibility frontier at any point represents the firm's opportunity cost. It is the decrease in output *A* required to produce one additional unit of *B*.

For a profit-maximizing firm we can determine the efficient (optimal) levels of *A* and *B*. For each combination of *A* and *B* that the firm produces, there is a corresponding level

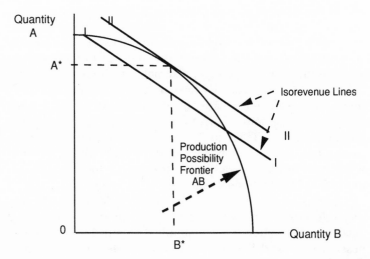

FIGURE 1   *Efficiency of a Firm*

of total revenue. This comes from adding the individual revenues from selling goods A and B, that is, $\pi_T = \pi_A + \pi_B = (p_A)$ $(A) + (p_B) (B)$, where the π's are revenues and the p's are given market prices. If we fix the revenue level π_T, we can find all the combinations of A and B that give this fixed level. This defines one isorevenue line, and varying π_T defines a whole family of isorevenue lines.

Given its production possibility frontier (PPF), a profit-maximizing firm wants to be on the highest feasible isorevenue line. Since the PPF assumes that inputs, and hence costs, are fixed, maximum profit requires the firm to lie on the highest feasible isorevenue curve—that is, the one just tangent to the PPF.[9] In figure 1 the firm reaches maximum profit at the tangency of isorevenue line I and the PPF, AB. It produces A^* and B^*. However, since this is a static model, discovery of an efficient point does not tell us whether the firm was efficient in the past or how it acquired the technologies and capital inputs it uses efficiently to produce final goods A and B in the present. Nor does this model tell us what the firm should do to be sure it has appropriate technology or capital goods in the future.

THE CASE OF A BUREAU

Suppose a bureau instead of a firm produces goods A and B. Assume that it has the same production possibility frontier as the firm, for this curve is presumably technologically determined.[10] Bureaus usually have no profit function to maximize. If we assume they are organizations like firms, we can say they define some "effectiveness" function they would like to maximize. Then, to be efficient the bureau in figure 2 should operate at the tangency of the isoeffectiveness curve with the production possibility frontier, as, for example, at point 1 on isoeffectiveness curve I.

There are two complications. First, the locus of any bureau's isoeffectiveness curves is quite uncertain. Effectiveness is not self-evident. For example, in figure 2, isoeffectiveness curves I and II intersect. If curve I were the true one, then the bureau would be efficient at point 1 on the produc-

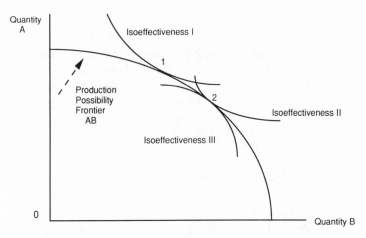

FIGURE 2   *Ambiguous Efficiency of Bureaus*

tion possibility frontier. If curve II were the true one, then the
bureau would be efficient at point 2 on curve II. Isoeffectiveness curves, for all we know, might be concave to the origin,
as is isoeffectiveness curve III. If this were the case, a bureau
could increase its effectiveness by deciding to deliver only A
or only B. Firms can experiment with different combinations
of A and B until they reach an efficient point. Bureaus have
less leeway to do so, since legislation and constituent pressures frequently restrict them to producing relatively fixed
amounts of A and B over time.

Public decision makers use a variety of devices to reveal
and check their beliefs about effectiveness. Periodically they
provide posture statements for staff and public consumption
that give the decision makers' view of their current and prospective environment and of how well production matches
the environment. They ask outside experts and sometimes
the public to comment on their current missions and on others they might invent or seize from someone else. Ex post,
they sometimes carry out evaluations to see how well programs have succeeded in relation to the objectives they selected. Still, there is no easy way for decision makers to
determine which of many possible curves should be used.

Since curves probably overlap, as in figure 2, a bureau can easily choose the wrong one. In other words, bureaus can be efficient at doing the wrong things, but the signals they get about erroneous behavior are highly ambiguous.

Bureaus usually have more than one objective. Figure 3 shows a bureau with two linear isoeffectiveness curves, labeled I and II. Suppose goods A and B are necessary for delivering both health and education services. The linear isoeffectiveness curve I shows the maximum level of education that can be achieved with feasible combinations of A and B. Isoeffectiveness curve II shows the maximum amount of health that can be achieved with feasible combinations of A and B. The different tangency points for the isoeffectiveness curves I and II show that when the bureau optimizes health it cannot optimize educational service, and vice versa. However, it can maximize health and accept a lower level of education as in curve I'. Or it can specify some acceptable lower bound for education as in curve I". If so, at point H, it maximizes health and achieves a satisfactory level of education, that is, amounts greater than those on curve I". Clearly, the bureau's constituents and clients will have different

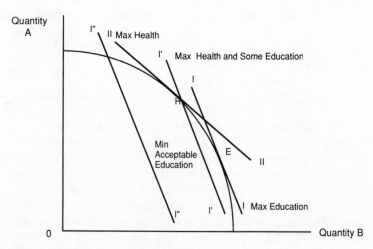

FIGURE 3   *Bureaus with Multiple Objectives*

views on the levels of health and education it should provide, as will its staff and sponsors, so that achieving static
efficiency becomes a complex bargaining process rather than
just a simple one of ensuring that objectives are consistent
with technologically determined constraints.[11]

DYNAMIC EFFICIENCY

The gains that firms obtain from achieving static efficiency
are probably less than those they can achieve by pushing
their current production possibility frontiers continuously
outward or by inventing new frontiers. They do the first by
inventing new process technologies, and they do the second
by introducing new products. Firms able to do this continuously are said to be *dynamically efficient*. To be dynamically
efficient, an organization has to invest in R&D and be sensitive to its results, or it has to be quick on its feet in capturing
technology produced by rivals at home or abroad. In either
case it has to take a strategic, long-run view of its situation. It
has to be willing and able to wait for large gains in the long
run.[12]

Figure 4 shows a firm that is statically inefficient. Whatever production possibilities there are at any given time, it
does not take full advantage of them. It operates inside its
production possibility frontier, possibly because management devotes most of its attention to maintaining dynamic
efficiency. Yet it is dynamically efficient. Its production possibility frontier shifts out from *AB* to *A'B'* to *A"B"*.

The small circles 1, 2, and 3 below each production possibility frontier show the inefficient amounts of *A* and *B* the
firm is actually producing. At each point in time it could
earn additional profit operating on its then feasible production possibility frontier. However, if it remains dynamically
efficient, then the profits it reaps at the inefficient points will
eventually exceed the profits possible by achieving static
efficiency on a given production possibility frontier. For example, the profit on the isorevenue line passing through inefficient point 3 is greater than the profit at the efficient points
on the isorevenue lines tangent to *A'B'* and *A"B"*.

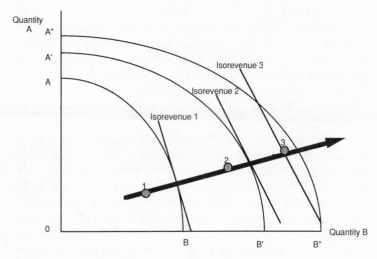

FIGURE 4 *Dynamic Efficiency*

Figure 5 shows a firm that can produce a new product (NEW). Prior to the introduction of output NEW, all of the firm's resources could only be put into producing an old product (OLD). With only one product, the production possibility frontier is the line *OJ* on the Y-axis, that is, *OJ* is the maximum OLD output possible given available resources and old technology. Now the invention of a technology that permits production of both OLD and NEW product creates a *potential* new production possibility frontier *TT*. On the potential *TT*, maximal OLD production would be less than *J*, since some of the resources once available for producing OLD will have to be used up in creating the NEW technology. If the firm invests in R&D, is successful, and also makes the required downstream investments, it will acquire the option of producing NEW as well as OLD output.[13]

The firm can maximize potential profit along the isorevenue line *EE*, but this may be too low to induce it to invest. Other firms can acquire the technology for producing NEW or find alternate technologies to do so. Profits may not then cover the costs of inventing and producing NEW, and

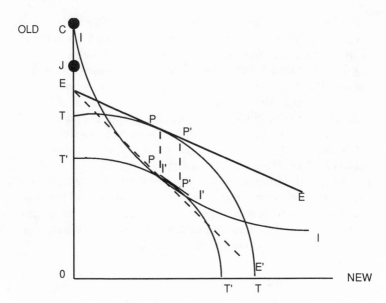

FIGURE 5   *Inventing a New Product*

therefore society may have to give firms special incentives. Suppose society gives the firm a patent that allows the firm to sell NEW for some higher price represented by isorevenue line *EE'*. The line *PP'* then becomes the firm's revenue measured in OLD product.

Now, *OJ* is the amount of OLD output before the technology was invented. *OT* is the amount of OLD that can now be produced. *OJ−OT* is the cost of the NEW technology in OLD output. Returns to the innovating firm must at least cover the OLD resources used up to create the NEW technology. So long as *PP'* ≥ *OJ−OT*, inventing NEW will be profitable.

Are consumers better off with NEW coming on the market? Let II be the indifference curve of some representative consumer. II would be tangent to the effective production possibility frontier, *T'T'* at *P'*. The concavity of the production possibility frontier implies that II must intersect the *Y*-axis at a point above *J*. Point *C* is the amount of OLD output the consumer feels is just worth the combination of OLD and

NEW she can now consume. Given the convexity of indifference curves and the concavity of the production possibility frontier, the consumer will be better off than when consuming only *OJ*. Once NEW is invented, the consumer gains the amount *CT*. It is the total gain *CT'* less the firm's profit *PP'*.

Even though the consumer would be better off if NEW technology were invented, the outcome is not statically efficient. Since the slopes of *EE* and *EE'* are necessarily different, consumers could get to an even higher indifference curve on *T'T'*. They could consume more NEW and still be able to pay the inventing firm the necessary *PP*, say, at *P'P'* on *I'I'*. Any device society uses to give inventors and innovators incentives to invest in new technology creates some element of monopoly. Thus society creates or designs a trade-off between dynamic efficiency and static efficiency.

Market Structures and Static and Dynamic Efficiency

If an economy were characterized entirely by perfectly competitive, profit-maximizing firms, it would attain static efficiency in production. However, economic history and econometrics both suggest that the welfare gains from being dynamically efficient are much greater than those from being statically efficient. Harberger (1954) originally estimated all the losses from allocative inefficiency to be about .1 percent of U.S. GNP. Such a low estimate triggered a round of criticism and corrections. Cowling and Mueller (1978) estimated 13 percent when they tried to account for costs devoted to creating monopolistic profits. In contrast, most of the historical gains in welfare have been attributed to technological advance. Obviously, an economy that grows at any positive rate will eventually surpass one that is not growing but has succeeded in eliminating all inefficiencies.

Comparing firms and markets in terms of their dynamic efficiency is a difficult task. The market structure that generates the most R&D, let alone the most innovation, remains an open question. Some economists have suggested that society in general underinvests in R&D but that competitive markets deliver more than noncompetitive ones. Others argue that market structures with monopoly elements may deliver more. Monopolies can capture the full benefits of an innovation, although they may not want to, for reasons of attracting entry or government scrutiny. And they presumably have the revenues for investment in R&D to generate innovation.[14]

Some degree of static inefficiency seems to be necessary for dynamic efficiency. There must be sufficient competition to provide incentives to innovate, but not so much that imitation dissipates benefits too quickly. Obviously, there may be trade-offs between the static efficiency provided by a competitive system (in equilibrium) and other economic structures that are not as efficient but innovate more.[15]

"INVISIBILITY"

To keep transaction and coordination costs down, a strategy or process should result in some socially desired end without any of the actors having to concern themselves with the end. With invisible strategies, each actor pursues his or her own objectives without worrying about anyone else's. Implicit rules and structures result in socially desired outcomes. Thus perfectly competitive markets provide overall production and consumption efficiency without anyone having to worry about attaining them (except possibly the bureaus that operate the infrastructure that supports the market).

The policy worth of invisible strategies goes beyond low transaction and coordination costs. From the perspective of permitting free choice, individual adjustments to implicit social constraints and incentives are superior to those that involve direct command and coercion. From a bureaucratic perspective, invisibility makes decision makers less vulnerable to blame and counterattack for unpopular decisions. Employing an invisibility criterion weights choices toward marketlike strategies, for there are very few other invisible strategies to be found.[16]

ROBUSTNESS

Despite the best forecasts and plans, strategies will frequently have to operate in environments for which they were not designed. Robust strategies operate reasonably well in such situations.

Figure 6 illustrates robustness schematically. Strategy B is more robust than A, because it functions better in a wider range of environments. It is less vulnerable than A to shifts in environment, although, as drawn, A has superior effectiveness to B in some restricted environments.

Most public decision makers are averse to risk, and thus, other things being equal, they would prefer robust strategies. Maximum performance in some restricted environment generally has less value than adequate performance in a wide range of environments. Given robustness, the decision maker can worry less about designing corrigibility into policy strategies, since robust ones will need less correction.

TIMELINESS

As bureaus in the United States are currently structured, time matters and is scarce. In the classic policy science portrait, decision makers confront constant demands for swift decisions, even if it is well known they will be imperfect. In the federal government the annual budget cycle always imposes some time pressure.[17] Administrations impose deadlines for solving problems to motivate staff. They say the mission of their agency depends on action or decision under time constraint. To get anything done under socially imposed time constraints, large-scale mobilization of resources in a very short time may be necessary, and those resources may have to be deployed without concerns about cost or efficiency.[18]

In fighting real wars or metaphorical ones over social or economic problems, showing some results in a short time is important to maintain support and momentum. For example, in the 1960s, the National Aeronautics and Space Administration (NASA) spent about $20 billion to get men to the

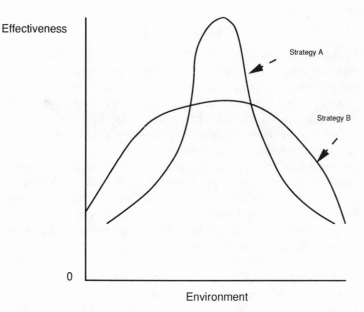

FIGURE 6   *Robust versus Nonrobust Strategies*

moon and back under a ten-year time constraint, but no doubt without a presidential time constraint the cost would have been less. More efficient boosters would have become available, and the technologies required for a moon shot would have been refined.

A striking recent example of decision makers' need for timeliness is the shift from centralized planning in the Soviet Union to a more market-oriented system. As Gorbachev's reforms take hold, an economy that is neither centrally planned nor yet market driven may, for a time, perform worse after reform than it did before. Ruling elites and the population can wait only so long before trying other leadership.

However, timeliness may matter the most in democratic political systems. In these, recognition and definition of the problem and consensus on a solution are all slow. But once problems and alternate solutions are recognized, society will reward decision makers for fast action.

STAKEHOLDER EQUITY

Gains and losses in efficiency are difficult to see. But policy winners and losers are highly visible. Every decision or program affects stakeholders and constituents. To be feasible, a strategy must therefore be seen as fair. Fair here means not that outcomes or even opportunity should be equal but rather that decisions or allocations are roughly acceptable to principal stakeholders and constituents.

Acceptability usually requires negotiation. Even though most formulas do not provide equal shares, negotiations give most shareholders some share. For example, revenue-sharing formulas in the 1970s contained factors for size of jurisdiction and revenue-raising effort. Both large and small jurisdictions could get some resources, and as a result the program remained acceptable. Giving something desirable for most principals retains the feasibility of a strategy. There is no guarantee, however, that equitable strategies will also turn out to be efficient. Political pressure for equity runs high, but demand for efficiency is generally low. Thus equity frequently may well be weighted more heavily than efficiency.

CORRIGIBILITY

Most programs and policies will produce some harmful consequences, despite efforts to avoid them before the policy is implemented. Thus corrigibility needs to be preserved. A bureau should learn something about its operations, and lessons learned can be applied to corrigible strategies.[19] However, strategies that are overly corrigible will deliver outcomes that do not resemble the intentions of their designers. For example, in the design and procurement of military aircraft, it is common for high level decision makers to want cheap, no-frills aircraft to avoid unfavorable quality-quantity trade-offs. The system for aircraft design and procurement permits innumerable changes in such a specification as stakeholders make their own corrections and additions but do not remove those of other stakeholders. The outcome of these multiple attempts at corrigibility is high-cost, gold-plated aircraft that do not meet the original intent or specifications.[20]

In the extreme, overly corrigible programs do not survive. Society learns to live with most of its current problems, and new problems and crises constantly erupt. Over time, there will be pressure to stop ongoing policies and programs, however cost-effective, for solving problems, and with the liberated resources to start new ones more relevant to the problems now pressuring decision makers.

ACCEPTABILITY

Strategies may well, ex ante, appear to be efficient, effective, and robust but remain politically infeasible. Most agree, for instance, that income maintenance or negative income tax programs are a more efficient way to handle public welfare than the way it is now done, but political support for these alternatives is simply not there. In the worst case, from a bureaucratic perspective, intended beneficiaries may themselves find decision makers' proposed strategies unacceptable—for example, when the Kennedy administration proposed to subsidize R&D for the housing industry, construction firms objected.[21]

On the other hand, it is relatively easy to design acceptable strategies, but they may fail with respect to other criteria. Strategies that spread resources thinly across all beneficiaries, for example, will generally be acceptable, even though each allocation is below the minimum size required to be effective.

Decision makers can sometimes create more support for currently unacceptable strategies through education and communication. Franklin Roosevelt was able to persuade the public and the Congress that Lend-Lease to Britain at the beginning of World War II was in the national interest, but all accounts suggest that he did not want to move too far ahead of what was publicly acceptable. Designing acceptable programs that retain other desirable attributes remains a tough challenge.

SIMPLICITY

Strategies that are simple and understandable on their face and impose low information requirements in the administrative process are generally preferable. Complexities require bureaus to make determinations and findings in particular cases. These then have to be coordinated and discussed up and down the line. If a strategy involves other bureaus, there has to be interagency coordination and agreement, a process that absorbs scarce time and reduces the freedom of the originating bureau.

Where a strategy requires complex and layered information to be effective, it is unlikely that bureaus will have the staff or the detailed expertise for prudent judgment. They can always try to buy missing expertise in the open market, but procurement of expert services is hedged by so many legal and accounting requirements that timeliness is inevitably lost, possibly along with other desired properties.

COST

All bureaus are constrained by budget and staff. Though they strive to avoid these constraints or to have them removed, at any given time they operate under some kind of cost constraint. While most bureaus are not consciously cost minimizers, any strategy's cost will have to fall within the budget that sponsors are willing to make available. Pursuing strategies that are clearly beyond any foreseeable budget creates suspicion about the intent of a bureau, its competence, or both.

JUDGING COMPLETE STRATEGIES

Few strategies will dominate all others, that is, that will be superior on every criterion. And some things may be so important to have that decision makers are willing to tolerate strategies with many undesirable outcomes. How, then, should strategies be compared? If, on balance, some appear to have equal merit, we can always appeal to higher-order criteria currently excluded from the appraisal calculus. For example, the delivery of justice, provision for democratic choice, or public dialogue might all be higher-order criteria that could be used to differentiate strategies. However, such appeals raise the possibility of an infinite regress and run into the constraint of timeliness.

A doctrine of sufficiency should probably hold. If one is left to choose between strategies that look reasonable or sufficient on five, ten, or twenty important criteria, then it may not matter that we miss choosing the very best among them. We can try some that are apparently adequate. Most, if not all, of the warranted alternatives will be somewhat corrigible. Information about the strategies that were forgone, together with the empirical and subsequent factual information about the operations of the one selected, can be used to make adjustments along the way.

USE OF THE TEN CRITERIA

Chapters 3–9 describe common strategies in political economy, how they work, and how they may fail in relation to the ten criteria. Chapter 11 employs the criteria to make an overall assessment of each strategy.

Chapter 3
The Roles of Markets

MARKETS PLAY multiple roles in economic decision making. They provide the signals and information that consumers and producers need. They furnish the incentives and "coercion" that make independent consumer and producer decisions consistent with each other. Through the distribution of monetary gains and losses, they confirm some private decisions and invalidate others, thereby suggesting paths for economic change, growth, and development. However, markets can play some of these roles badly or not at all. They can fail.

This chapter reviews the conditions necessary for market systems to do their work reasonably well and discusses different types of market failure. Static market failures are barriers or conditions that prevent an economy from attaining allocative or technical efficiency at a given time. Static market failures provide necessary conditions for policy intervention.[1] This chapter also describes dynamic market failures— public or private barriers to innovation—which have become a matter of special policy concern in the United States.[2] The last part of the chapter appraises the use of markets in solving public policy problems using the criteria defined and discussed in chapter 2.

WHAT IS A MARKET?

A market is a social arrangement that permits voluntary exchange of privately provided goods and services with known or discoverable attributes. Although modern markets may be

26

traced back to medieval town fairs, they need not 1 fixed place.[3] For example, highly dispersed electroni(kets are becoming more common as communications and computer technology become more integrated.

Every market has a transactions language, which, in a market with large numbers of buyers and sellers, can be spare. Buyers and sellers can get by with a relatively simple price-quantity language.[4] For large classes of goods and services, the market infrastructures designed by government present sufficient information about quality. For example, the government certifies the octane in gas or the quality of meat or wheat. If buyers or sellers lack information about prices or quantities, they can get it through low-cost queries of other buyers or sellers.[5] Bargaining can thus be restricted to statements about acceptable prices and quantities.[6]

In every market, economic theory assumes that traders pursue their own self-interest. If maximizing utility motivates consumers and maximizing profits motivates firms, then relative prices and their fluctuation determine quantities bought or sold. Once everyone understands the quantitative and qualitative attributes of goods and services proposed in trade, they need only know relative prices to carry out their own optimizing calculations. On the basis of relative prices, they make offers and counteroffers. When there is inconsistency between the buying and selling prices, relative prices change, and traders recalculate. Eventually relative prices emerge that are consistent simultaneously with all offers and counteroffers, and markets clear—that is, exchange takes place.[7] Such exchange rations the current supply of goods. Consumers who place the value of a good at a price higher than its market clearing price get the good. Sellers, at a minimum, get back their costs of production.

Market systems do not require any notions of consumers' sovereignty for their operation. However, in Western economies a rough consensus exists that the purpose of production is to satisfy individual and collective consumer wants. Consumers, in principle, give producers the mix or menu of goods and services they want.[8] Given this menu, markets

give firms the incentives to deliver the desired mix at least
social (opportunity) cost.

HISTORICAL DEVELOPMENT

Market systems today are the preferred means of allocating
resources in most nations. Even those with a strong tradition of central planning have discovered that markets are
superior to planning. Most East European countries are dis-
mantling their planning bureaucracies. The Soviet Union's
perestroika or restructuring is an attempt to inject market
incentives and flexibility into a highly centralized, inefficient economy. Since the death of Mao, China has reintro-
duced private markets in agriculture and is trying to extend
their use to industry.[9]

Nevertheless, market *systems* are a relatively late social
invention. Individual markets have existed as long as civiliza-
tion.[10] However, in classical and feudal economies, neither
the satisfaction of consumer wants nor productive efficiency
was an explicit or socially agreed objective. There was no
social consensus that market systems served useful purposes
or, if there was consensus, the underlying political, legal,
and organizational conditions could not be met.[11]

Starting from a feudal base, it took a long time to develop
attitudes and institutions favorable to the formation of market
systems. Necessary individual rights to own and exchange
property were not well established. At first, emerging nation-
states were too weak to create the needed rights and exchange
structures. Nor did they view this creation of property rights
and economic structures for the private sector as one of their
major functions. Then, when their power grew, they regulated
economic activity, hampering the mobility of capital and labor and controlling opportunities for entrepreneurship.

The emergence of extensive market systems for products
and factors coincides with the Industrial Revolution, which
made possible the large-scale production of goods and services whose quantity and quality could be measured. At the
very same time, the concept of personal property rights
gained greater acceptance. A more powerful, central state

was now able and willing to define legitimate rights to property, and it stood ready to enforce contracts for the exchange of property.[12]

By the twentieth century, the power of the state to regulate, control, and plan market activity increased significantly. The Great Depression and two world wars inevitably increased the role of the state in economic affairs. Many Western economies today employ some weak form of central planning, though private market exchange remains the dominant form of transaction. Indeed, Western nations that experimented with planning and public ownership of production—for example, Great Britain—have been busy privatizing their economies. Recent attempts at decentralization in Eastern Europe, the Soviet Union, and China provide graphic evidence of planning failure, of the allocative and technical inefficiency resulting from strong central planning strategies applied over long periods.

THEORY OF MARKETS

Market systems are supposed to bring production decisions into line with consumer preferences at any one time and across time. We have a well-developed, highly stylized theory of how market systems do this. Suppose that the economy is in a general equilibrium[13] and that there is a shift in preferences among existing goods and services. Prices fall in some markets and rise in others and serve as signals to current and prospective producers. Their interest in maximum profit would be well served if they shifted their inputs from lines of production where demand was falling to lines where it was rising.

Existing firms find it easy to make this shift because, by assumption, they employ only highly mobile and adaptive factor inputs. If, for some reason, such shifts result in persistent losses for some firms, they shut down and release the inputs they have been using. Newly released inputs flow easily to the old and new firms that can now use them best—that is, where their marginal products are highest. Given the price shifts, marginal products and profits will now be higher in markets where prices are rising.

Since all firms pursue every possible way to increase their profits in the long run, they search out the least costly way to produce the changed output mix, given currently available technology. Some firms may be more efficient than others in the short run; in the long run, every firm can imitate the most efficient ones, and there are no barriers to imitation. Provided that the private and social costs of changing the product mix are identical or that government can make them so via appropriate taxes and subsidies, some new equilibrium is reached where increased consumer demand is again satisfied at the least possible social cost for the changed output.[14]

Figure 7 shows a stylized process for a constant cost industry, one where the cost curves of firms do not shift up or down as entry occurs. This industry is in equilibrium at P^*, Q^*. Demand, for some reason, shifts up from D to D'. In the short run, firms start making abnormal profits and increase

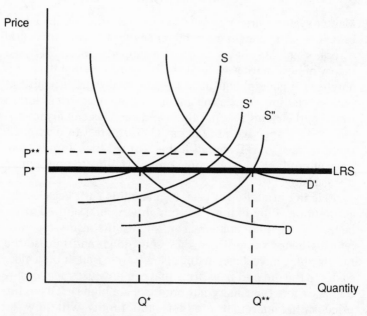

FIGURE 7   *Demand-induced Supply Shift (Constant Cost Industry)*

their output and profits. Increased profits attract entry both by firms operating in other industries and by new starts. The short-run supply curve shifts outward from S to S'. However, the short-run equilibrium price P^{**} still provides abnormal profits. Entry continues until these are wiped out at the new equilibrium P^*, Q^{**}. The long-run supply curve is the solid line at P^*. The point is that if consumers decide they want more Q, over the long run they get what they want at the least social cost.

Though the speed of these adjustments is not determined within the theory, the implicit assumption is that adjustments are rapid. An economic system that takes very long to adjust to changing circumstances would not have much power to persuade politicians or the public that its operations should be left alone rather than politically altered. Hence any sluggishness observed in actual markets is the result of social and political barriers to the adjustment process: government, unions, or other institutions retard the necessary adjustments.[15]

The political message inherent in using market systems is that all barriers that prevent correct and rapid price signals and responses should be removed. If static efficiency is the aim, then government policies and programs should be directed toward rooting out barriers to competition. If the economy were perfectly competitive, any equilibrium it eventually reached would be statically efficient (Pareto-efficient).[16] If government has equity concerns, then it should try to satisfy them through means that do not affect market-determined relative prices. Government should make equity judgments by shifting income in lump sums and letting the market determine an efficient allocation given the equity adjustment.[17]

THE INNOVATION PROCESS

Static efficiency is not the only, or even the chief, criterion for judging the performance of economic systems. Given our strong beliefs in production for consumer welfare, the innovative capabilities of any economic system are perhaps even more important. An economy can tolerate large amounts of static inefficiency if it continually generates new products and invents cost-reducing processes. In fact, some economists have argued that there is a trade-off between efficiency and innovation.[18] An economy that was efficient all the time would exhaust all opportunities for windfall profits. However, it is just the chance of such profits that motivates the search for new products or processes.[19]

A stylized version of the innovation process in a market system runs as follows. Current and prospective entrepreneurs keep track of the information produced by science and technology and try to determine how that information can eventually be embodied in a product or process.[20] They also collect information about the prospective needs of users—other producers and consumers—in some systematic way. Given an evident match between the two streams of information, they decide to "translate" or "congeal" their information into new goods and services or cost-reducing processes.[21] Having done this, they expose the newly developed goods and processes to various market tests, which connect the discoveries of science and technology to the demands of users. Thus successful innovation eventually requires both the push of technology and the pull of demand.[22]

Only some new products and processes survive market tests, because entrepreneurs can be quite fallible about costs and demand. This is why risk taking is said to be the core of entrepreneurial activity. From a social perspective, if enough risks are taken, very few potential innovations will be overlooked, so market systems pay high rewards for successful risk taking. If one entrepreneur misreads technological possibilities, then another will make the correct reading. And if one entrepreneur misreads prospective user demand, then another will make the correct estimate.

Once new products and processes become widely diffused, they generate corollary changes in demand for both old and new goods and services and for factors of production. These induced changes create additional opportunities for profit, and the innovation process continues.[23] In this way society's menu of goods and services stays closely articulated with changing technological capabilities and consumers' definitions of their needs.

POLICY IMPLICATIONS OF TECHNOLOGICAL CHANGE

If society wants innovation, the main policy message is that legal and institutional obstacles to innovation in the market system should be removed. The range of such impediments in the United States is large, from antitrust laws, or perhaps their legal and administrative interpretation, to some forms of social regulation. The impacts on innovation, being diffuse, are rarely considered when laws are passed or regulations are set, so it is easy to produce unintended adverse impacts on the innovation process.

However, this message is never as clear or strong as the call for getting rid of barriers to static efficiency. The optimal market structure for innovation is not known. It may well involve significant elements of inefficiency. Market structures that lie somewhere between perfect competition and monopoly may well be the most innovative,[24] and no one has yet found structures that are reasonable from the standpoint of both innovation and efficiency.

When public policy tries to account for both efficiency and innovation, there are complex trade-offs. Patents, as was noted in chapter 2, create monopolies and hence some welfare losses. However, public disclosure via a patent of some of the information held by inventing or innovating firms can be of significant value to their rivals and to the public, eventually increasing welfare. Similarly, pooling and sharing of technical information by rivals in an industry may reduce competition and incentives for efficiency, but it might enhance innovation. There is no way to make an a priori choice about policies that simultaneously affect innovation potential and efficiency, especially where an increase in one conceivably decreases the other.

MARKET FAILURE AT A GIVEN TIME

Actual markets rarely operate smoothly, and frequently they fail, which means that for some reason they do not provide efficient outcomes. There are at least five major technical reasons for market failure at any given time.

Natural Monopoly and Increasing Returns

There may be increasing returns to scale (decreasing unit costs) in the production of some socially important goods. If scale economies are very large, then monopoly may be preferable to competitive delivery, for it provides desired output at lower social cost. However, monopolies are allocatively inefficient. If government were to try to impose the marginal cost pricing that would be socially efficient, a decreasing cost monopolist would suffer losses and eventually leave the industry. Not having socially desired output would itself be a cost.

Public subsidy is one alternative. It raises significant questions about the distribution of benefits and costs between the general taxpayer and consumers of the monopolist's output. Regulation is another alternative. It raises complex questions about the information that is obtainable about the monopolist's costs and the rules the regulator should use. In principle, regulatory commissions use average cost pricing, which strikes some balance between the savings derived from maximum-scale economies and those from allocative efficiency. In practice, since pricing is a bargaining process, there is the chance of "commission failure" whereby neither economies of scale nor efficiency is realized. Public ownership is a third alternative, but it creates the risk of bureaucratic failure. For example, publicly owned utilities may be less efficient than privately held ones. There is less market pressure but more social objectives to satisfy.

Public Goods

Not all socially important products and services have the necessary characteristics for efficient production by firms and markets. In particular, if profit-making firms cannot prevent those unwilling to pay for a product from consuming it, they will have no incentives to produce. They have to recover costs.

National defense is the most commonly used example.

Citizens consume the deterrent and war-fighting services provided by the military whether they pay for them or not. Unless taxed to pay for these services, citizens are free riders. Lighthouses are another commonly used, if not completely accurate, example. Once in operation, a lighthouse cannot limit its services just to paying ships. Any passing ship can ride free. Since the costs of producing light cannot be covered by sale, prospective lighthouse firms will not invest in providing the service, even though society collectively would be better off with fewer shipwrecks.[25]

On the demand side, the use of lighthouse service by one passing ship in no way prevents other ships from using it. The light—or, more accurately, the information provided by the light—is nondepletable or nonrival. So, were a lighthouse to be built, the information about sea and coast that it produced should be diffused to all ships that wanted it at the (marginal) cost of transmission. Pareto efficiency requires that anyone who can benefit from nondepletable goods or services should receive them. However, since lighthouses eventually wear out, replacement costs would not be covered by such a policy, and so we face a problem in dynamics.

A prospective lighthouse industry might be a candidate for policy intervention. For example, government could tax all ships operating in its territorial waters. It could use the proceeds to provide the service, either publicly or privately, through subsidy of lighthouse companies. Alternately, it could use general tax funds to do R&D on technologies that would trigger the light only if users paid; or, by appropriate incentive—say, an R&D investment tax credit—it could encourage private firms to undertake the R&D. Successful R&D would turn the public good into a private one. Government support of R&D to benefit the private sector has a long history—for example, in agriculture, aircraft, and electronics. However, the rules for providing it remain controversial.[26]

Externalities

Externalities are divergences between private and social costs or benefits. Given such divergences, there will be either too little or too much production or consumption.[27] A production externality exists when the production function of one firm is influenced by the actions of another firm or entity, but such actions are not mediated by any market price. The firm obtains benefits or absorbs costs as a result of someone else's decisions. For example, until recently, even though pollution is a joint output of most production processes, it never entered anyone's profit-maximizing calculus very strongly. Pollution had zero private cost, from the standpoint of producers. However, it imposed environmental and health costs on society. Thus the price of goods produced by polluters did not reflect their true social opportunity cost, which made for inefficient economic outcomes.

The policy problem here is finding cost-effective ways to "internalize" externalities or, at least, to force the parties involved to account for them. Government does this with information, regulations, standards, assignments of property rights, or taxes and subsidies. Letting firms adjust to market prices (costs) corrected in some way for externalities is the cheapest possible method of handling them. Economists also argue that correcting the price system is superior to other alternatives in preserving individual choice and social flexibility.[28] However, price strategies may not be administratively or politically feasible.

Consumption externalities exist when an individual's utility is influenced by some other individual's utility, but this dependence is not mediated by any price. For example, education of all citizens may increase one's quality of life or the quality of the civic culture, increasing utility, but the price system has difficulty accounting for such impacts. Thus markets may underproduce education. Government programs and policies to deal with consumption externalities raise questions of efficiency and effectiveness just as production externalities do, but they often raise questions of appropriateness as well. At least in the United States, education is a state and local function, not a federal one, so that if the federal government wants to design programs to improve education, these must account for its being provided locally. Handling consumption externalities raises jurisdictional and ethical issues that are less prominent in dealing with production externalities.

The standard cure for externalities is taxes and subsidies designed to make private costs and social costs equal. If government has good information about costs and demand, it can set taxes in such a way as to eliminate the externality. Figure 8 shows two stylized cases. In the left-hand diagram the marginal social cost of output is greater than marginal private cost. Given good information, government imposes a tax on producers such that the new effective supply curve (PMC + TAX) passes through the point where the marginal social benefit (demand curve) just intersects the marginal social cost. Purely private production and consumption decisions now result in socially optimal output. In the right-hand diagram the marginal private benefits of output are less than marginal social benefits, so the government provides a subsidy that makes the marginal private benefits intersect the point where marginal social benefit is equal to marginal social cost (and private cost in this case).

Asymmetries in Information

Competitive markets work well when all parties hold just the right amounts of information about the quantity and quality of goods and services offered. When this is the case, all available possibilities for utility and profit maximization can be exhausted. Given that the other conditions hold, the economy will move to some efficient equilibrium. There are many products whose quantity, quality, or other attribute important to buyers may be difficult to determine. When there are asymmetries in information, some exchanges that would be socially beneficial will not be made.

The used car market is an often cited example.[29] Consumers have no easy way of distinguishing used cars that are lemons from those that provide decent transportation. Though they might rely on the seller's reputation, in many cases this is also unknown. Without precise information on a particular car or particular seller, the most reasonable assumption is that any given car is of average quality. Therefore, consumers offer an average price. But owners of above-average cars are not

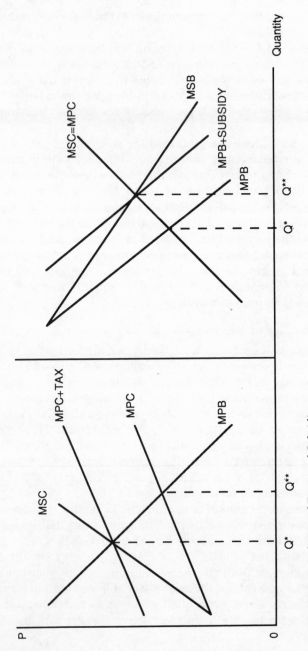

FIGURE 8 Social Uses of Taxes and Subsidies

willing to sell at average price, and they withdraw their cars from the market, with the result that the average quality of the used car population declines. This decline induces even lower offers from buyers, leading to further declines in quality. Ultimately, the market disappears.

Such an asymmetry can be overcome by discovering some way to signal the quality of a particular car. Buyers may make their offers contingent on a warrant by an expert mechanic; or they may try to present a credible threat of retaliation should the car they buy turn out to be unsatisfactory. The state may stand behind their threat with "lemon laws" or other forms of support.

In the case of used cars, sellers know more than buyers. However, in many markets sellers know less than buyers. Health insurers, for example, cannot usually know more about the health of their customers than customers themselves know. So buyers of health insurance can select themselves into plans that promise them the most benefits. However, the ex post costs of handling larger numbers than anticipated of self-selected patients cannot be filtered into the original price of the insurance. So costs may not cover revenues, or prices may rise. As prices rise, healthy subscribers leave, and the insuring company is left with proportionately high-risk subscribers and requires further cost increases. However, obtaining more accurate information on the health of the insuring population can itself be costly or difficult.

Missing Markets

It may be impossible or very costly to form markets for some goods and services. In allocating resources efficiently between the present and the future, we need many futures markets. Although some exist, they do not exist for every possible future contingency or for every good that may be socially important.

Government may try to create a missing market. For example, it could try to create a market for pollution rights by matching up those with a "need" to pollute with sellers holding state-granted rights to pollute. These sellers could be those who would suffer damage. Alternately, polluters could be given rights to pollute and could ask a price for not polluting.

There is a symmetry of theoretical outcomes given the right conditions.[30] Practically, it is frequently costly to form such markets. Those who suffer and cause pollution are often widely dispersed. The transactions costs of identifying polluters and true sufferers may be so great as to overcome any gains in efficiency from using a market.

INNOVATION FAILURES

Just as market systems may fail to be efficient, they may fail to be innovative. The reasons for failure to innovate are "softer," more institutional and organizational, and less technological than those responsible for failure to obtain efficiency at a given time.

Too Small a Research Base

Many innovations today derive from advances in basic research, which is very close to being a public good. In fact, to be worth much to science, research must be disseminated rapidly and widely. Scientific canons require that researchers not try to capture private benefits from their work. Private profit-making firms then have weak incentives to engage in basic research, even though it may pay over time, both privately and socially.

Although government can step in and fund such research, there are no algorithms that convincingly lead us to the optimal level and composition. In general, bureaus favor using public monies for activities that pay off modestly in the short run over research activities with high but uncertain future returns. So even with a strong government role, the research base may be too small, and its composition may be inappropriate. After a while, the stock of information that can be translated into new technologies declines: the rate of innovation eventually decreases because the economy does not produce enough new information.

High Risks and Costs

The costs and risks associated with some prospective socially desirable or necessary products may be too great for a private firm to undertake by itself. New, large-scale projects with unknown physical scaling effects and economics frequently encounter resistance even in very large private firms. Firms argue that such projects are beyond their individual capabilities and willingness to assume risk. If all firms in an industry take this view, then some socially valuable products or processes will be lost.

Applied R&D or demonstration programs sponsored by government may give a reluctant industry additional information and reduce risks and costs. For example, the electric power industry rejected nuclear power in its infancy, so the federal government decided to demonstrate its technical and economic feasibility. The government announced that this was done in 1953. Yet thirty-seven years later the government still finds itself involved in nuclear power.

In considering market corrections, government finds itself in a quandary. If the market makes some ex ante estimates that the returns from producing some product will be too low, this may be correct. Government then supports economic activity that does not meet a market test. Government's ex ante estimates of social returns may also be mistaken, and it may find itself supporting programs to benefit the private sector where both private and social returns are low; in addition, it becomes difficult to stop them.

Myopic Managers

Management may be very myopic about the future and highly oriented to maximizing short-run profits. For various reasons, managers may, ex ante, constantly estimate private rates of return to longer-run investments as too low, even though, ex post, private and social returns would be very high.[31] If so, their firms do not undertake enough R&D. Even with sufficient R&D, the investments required to bring some new product or process on line may be perceived as inordinately large. Managers may face intense pressure for short-run returns. If so, firms will not undertake enough long-run projects, and there will be insufficient variety.[32]

Inappropriate Market Structures

Competitive market systems eventually approach efficiency. However, industries that are highly competitive may not innovate enough because of the conditions that prevent them from exercising market power. Small individual firms will have difficulty raising resources for R&D, and any innovations they consider making can easily be imitated by other firms, which reduces the incentive to innovate. In the past the existence of "fragmented" industries has served as a rationale for government provision of some services to benefit industry. For example, the fragmented nature of U.S. agriculture in the nineteenth century was one reason for the extensive involvement of the federal government in basic and applied agricultural research.

In contrast to competitive firms, monopolies may have the resources for innovation, and, by definition, they can appropriate the benefits. But they may not have the incentives since there is no pressure from rivals. Of course, monopoly-destroying innovations coming from other industries may be a sufficient incentive.

There may, of course, be intermediate structures that permit sufficient capture of returns and yet retain sufficient competitive pressures to force firms to innovate.[33] However, if the choice of a market structure involves trade-offs between efficiency and innovation, among all the structures possible, no one knows the one that strikes a reasonable balance. No invisible hand guides an economy on the innovation dimension.

Gaps in Information

Information gaps may prevent innovation in production. For example, the aircraft industry may discover some process that could be applied to increase housing productivity. But the aircraft industry is not a traditional supplier of the housing industry, and therefore housing firms have little incentive to keep track of developments in aircraft construction. Conversely, suppliers traditionally carry out some R&D that improves the performance of their customers. However, the aircraft industry does not ordinarily think of itself as a supplier of products or information for the housing industry, and thus an information gap exists.

Such information gaps motivate the federal government's various attempts at designing civilian technology policy.[34] Bureaus may be called on to fill the gaps and provide some of the missing information linkages between industries. For they can receive mandates and resources to keep track of emerging information in various industries relevant to other industries, and they can disseminate such information. Nearly all civilian technology proposals for the U.S. economy include the provision of "generic" information.

Unbalanced Rights in New Information

In market systems there is a trade-off between the production of information and its use. Production of information by private firms requires exclusivity, but maximum social benefits accrue when information is accessible to all who want it. Once information is produced, it cannot be destroyed, and the cost of its dissemination is usually very low. Government determines the trade-off, since it defines property rights in information: as was noted earlier, to encourage the output of information, it provides limited protection to producers via the patent system and trade secret laws. In exchange, however, government requires the release of partial information about inventions that others may be able to use as clues, if not directly. The balance the government strikes between protection and disclosure strongly influences the ability of a market system to innovate. But no one knows the optimal degree of patent protection or trade secrecy.

Government Regulation

Environmental, health, and safety regulations may skew R&D portfolios toward "defensive" R&D to ensure compliance rather than "offensive" R&D oriented toward new products and processes. Regulatory processes may also cause significant delay in the construction of new plants embodying the latest technology, thereby reducing estimates of private returns.

The results of regulation, however, are not all negative. First, the inability of some industries and firms to comply with social regulation means that an opportunity must exist for others to pursue offensive R&D aimed at bringing effective technology for compliance to noncomplying industries and firms. Second, installing new technology and processes to ensure compliance may also increase productivity. Potential for compliance frequently comes bundled with productivity-increasing technology.

Economic regulation, although not specifically designed to do so, may have an impact on a firm's propensity to innovate. For example, regulation may reduce competition by controlling entry. However, the absence of entry and imitation may reduce the risk of innovation by existing firms. In the case of rate-of-return regulation, the firm may be induced to invest in capital-intensive (labor-augmenting) technology instead.

Overinvestment

Instead of underinvesting, firms may overinvest in R&D because they need to protect themselves against rivals. Consequently, they may plow resources into inventing very similar products or processes. If we think of research as a race to achieve a patent, then there may be too much research in one field and not enough in another.[35] Concentration on such rivalry may also generate innovation that is socially too early.

THE QUESTION OF EQUITY

Market systems, when well designed and operated, may provide efficient use of resources, and historically they have delivered high rates of innovation. They will not automatically provide equity or fairness, however. Lack of equity is not some technical market failure; it is a political judgment that some people or groups do not have enough voice in giving directions to the market. Markets are sensitive to what the currently wealthier members of society want, so that specifications of current output come from those whom the market has, in the past, rewarded with high income. From the perspective of equity, the market can be efficient at producing the wrong things.

The government may decide to make the distribution of wealth or income more equal, according to some principle of fairness. Alternately, it may seek to equalize the opportunity to gain higher income today so that some may have a greater voice in the future. Proposals for negative income taxes or income maintenance rest on the first principle, and affirmative action and technical training programs rest on the second.

IDENTIFYING A MARKET FAILURE

The identification of market failure can be very complex. A traditional illustration of an externality concerns the interactions between one beekeeper and one flower grower, producing side by side. It can be shown how, by suitably internalizing the mutual externalities, both can benefit.[36] However, if there are dozens or thousands of beekeepers and flower growers, internalization becomes difficult: how could one identify whose bees and flowers were creating externalities?

In recent years, externalities relating to pollution have been a prominent public issue. We can presumably discover pollution by pointing at it or smelling it. However, health and environmental damage may be subtle and difficult to detect and assign. Estimates of damage can be highly variable in either direction as empirical and theoretical knowledge builds up. For example, in the 1970s many held that the escape of fluorocarbons from aerosol cans into the atmosphere was depleting the ozone layer, which would lead to an increased incidence of skin cancer. The costs associated with getting and curing skin cancer, of course, were never included in the profit calculations of aerosol producers. However, demonstrating the existence and seriousness of the fluorocarbon externality is far removed from asserting that honey and flower production involve externalities or even asserting that effluents from a factory decrease the quality of water downstream.

The fluorocarbon externality rests on a complex and shifting network of scientific argument and evidence. It took the joint sifting and evaluation of evidence by technical experts and analysts and lengthy collective arguments to decide that this externality existed and was persistent and serious. So the existence of market failures, or more precisely, justified belief in their existence, frequently depends on complex, uncertain, and provisional scientific and technical arguments.

Reasonable people can differ about whether scientific evidence is strong enough to invoke some policy response. More sophisticated analysis may suggest later that failures are stronger or weaker than first suspected. Current policy and programs may then be maladapted or may even make things worse. However, standard schemes for correction generally provide little room for decision makers to hedge or experiment. Taxes and subsidies cannot be changed easily in proportion to changes in scientific and technical information, and standards create a web of expectation and action that is very costly to tear up.

MARKET FAILURE AND THE
ACTUAL CHOICE OF STRATEGY

In practice, the logic of market failure provides no clear guidance on the choice between public or private provision of goods and services or between regulation or additional incentives for the private sector. For most goods and services that concern government, decision makers usually encounter competing claims, each of reasonable merit, that delivery either by bureaus or by private firms is preferred. Advocates for each position exchange claims and counterclaims about the other. All claims are debatable, but the debates rarely prove that one strategy always dominates.

Decision makers can reasonably decide to choose one strategy over another without too much discomfort. Whatever they choose can usually be justified. If they choose to use bureaus, the justification does not necessarily correlate with the market failure. Government can always claim it needs to intervene in markets because of its own legitimate interests. For example, it is a dominant user of some output—tanks—and a dominant employer of some factors of production—scientists and engineers. It is the agent that is supposed to take care of national needs and national security. In any case, the notion of public goods in most advanced economies is broader than in the United States. There is less political discomfort when the state owns and runs railroads, TV stations, banks, and the like.

Occasionally governments justify programs by claiming they are themselves the cause of some externality. For example, public funds to subsidize the education of scientists and engineers are justified on grounds that the government imposes large, uncounted costs on the private, nondefense sector by employing so many technical personnel in the defense sector. Without the pull of the defense sector, more scientists and engineers would remain in the civilian sector doing R&D more applicable to civilian markets and producing higher-quality products.

Actual choices naturally define the scope of public and private interest. The portfolio of reasonably warranted activities that government elects to perform sets the boundaries between public and private provision and legitimates a particular division of goods and services. Once an economic activity has been defined as public, the private sector has fewer incentives to search for ways to privatize it. Conversely, if decision makers want to make some public activities private, operating bureaucracies and constituents will not easily give up programs they believe are legitimately public, even though no technological or economic barriers prevent them from being private.

An Appraisal of Markets as Problem-Solving Devices

Assume that a decision maker faces some social or environmental problem and there are several feasible strategies for attacking it—markets, regulated markets, public service delivery. Suppose also that policy designers suggest that setting up a competitive market is the preferred way to solve the problem.[37] Assuming a government capability and willingness to create fine-grained property and trading rights, and an appropriate low-cost infrastructure for supporting an emerging market, one can design a market mechanism to address almost any kind of problem. However, given the appraisal factors of chapter 2, how should decision makers evaluate their analysts' suggestions?

Obviously, how markets perform as a solution to noneconomic problems depends on detail and particular circumstances. Looking at our appraisal factors, we see that relatively competitive markets are very strong on static efficiency and invisibility. They are problematic on dynamic efficiency. A designer of markets might have to create special incentives or subsidies to prompt innovation. One can imagine having to set up a market to provide innovation for the primary problem-solving market, and the new innovation market might be inefficient, for it might well require monopoly elements.

The likelihood of unintended outcomes arising from markets is relatively high. Corrigibility and controllability to account for these will be low. Instead of retaining instruments that the decision maker can directly apply and control, substantive outcomes are determined by process, the constrained, interactive decisions of consumers and producers. The government cannot possibly know how they will perceive the a priori incentives it designs. Some of them will surely respond in unanticipated and surprising ways, and some will respond in ways contrary to the original policy objective.

Unintended results may require another round of government adjustments and corrections. For example, attempts to make medical markets efficient result in the exclusion of classes of people and illnesses whose presence reduces output per unit of input. But the excluded classes are the ones who need medical care the most. Treating sick people does not make for efficiency. In the face of this consequence, decision makers could design a new market, for example, a market in tradable health vouchers that would be given to those most ill. But this imposes requirements for identifying this class, and there are problems of adverse selection and moral hazard. This makes a market solution very complex and costly relative to the original problem. Frequent government adjustments and interventions are hard to implement, and they defeat the purposes of setting up a market in the first place.

Timeliness will always be critical in using markets to solve any policy problem. First, some problems have to be solved quickly because the social damage they inflict is high and increasing. Second, at least in federal service, most high-level decision makers have a short tenure, so that their personal gains from long-term solutions are slim. From an organizational perspective, proposals to solve a problem efficiently sometime in the future do not provide much increase in the things bureaus value. So early solutions are naturally preferred over later ones. In fact, market approaches have only a limited time to work. Even if all stakeholders agree initially to let a market take the time it needs, bureaus, stakeholders, and the public have short memories. Despite solemn agreements, a demand for short-run results inevitably emerges.

Certainly price increases necessary to equilibrate a market are not ordinarily considered signals that the market is working properly to relieve some restricted supply of goods and services. For example, while energy markets might well have adjusted to the oil shocks of 1973 and 1979 without any national attempts to set policy, the large-scale economic consequences meant that no decision maker could plausibly say that it was best to wait.

Reaching political consensus to solve a problem usually requires outcomes involving fair shares or roughly equal pain. However, the efficiency-inducing properties of the market mean unequal outcomes. Politically, demonstrating equity (fair share) is more important than cost-minimizing efficiency. To economists it is equitable to let firms that have a comparative advantage, say, in reducing pollution or improving their workplace, do more of it. However, if costs are going to be increased for some firms, then they may have to be increased for all; otherwise, some individuals or firms escape their perceived social responsibility for complying with socially approved regulation.

Permitting efficient but differential responses via market operations may simply generate political pressures that democratic governments are not well prepared to withstand. Government might as well pursue equitable programs that can be put into place quickly as efficient ones that cannot. Certainly, lack of political equity is easy to see and to point out to others. Efficiency, however, is very hard to observe. Neither the public nor the bureaucracy will know much about the comparative cost advantages of different firms as they respond to market incentives or are aware that the market is keeping overall social costs down.

Finally, some believe that market strategies have lower information and transaction costs than other strategies. There is no need for structures and organizations to channel the flow of information between public decision makers and private actors, but the market does require a substantial infrastructure to adjudicate property rights, set standards, and enforce contracts. There is no inherent guarantee that the costs of running markets are always lower than those required by competing strategies. Thus, even where a problem might be solved by defining property rights and creating markets, there is no hard evidence that markets dominate other problem-solving modes.

Chapter 4
The Microeconomics of Bureaus

THEORY AND popular reporting on bureaus in the last decade or so have focused on their disorders and diseases.[1] The study of effective, successful bureaus is less popular today than it was in the past—perhaps there are fewer successful bureaus.[2] A generation ago economists argued that public enterprises could and would give private industry lessons in efficient operations. The performance of state-owned utilities such as the Tennessee Valley Authority (TVA) would serve as the yardstick for measuring the performance of privately owned utilities. However, today economists believe that bureaus and public enterprise are inherently inefficient, whether their output consists of tangible goods and services or economic and social regulation.[3]

Only a few years ago, organizational analysts believed that government knew how to design and manage very large complex projects.[4] They believed that new planning and budgeting systems were going to rationalize defense strategies and procurement and that they would do the same for civilian programs. However, inefficiency plagues the defense sector to this day.[5] When the federal government applied newly developed planning and budgeting techniques to its domestic programs, they did not do the job they were supposed to. Perceptions of failure have helped create a ground swell for the privatization of many traditionally public activities and for the application of market principles to those activities not prime candidates for privatization.[6]

Views of bureaucratic failure come in at least two versions, weak and strong. The weak one is that bureaucracies fail because special interests control them and incompetents run them. Their main product is inefficient delivery of poorly designed services, unnecessary red tape, and unproductive regulation. If this version were true, then we could improve performance by hiring better people or simplifying procedures. We could provide additional incentives and safeguards to ensure efficiency and prevent capture by interest groups and constituents.

A stronger, more sophisticated view of bureaucratic failure is symmetric with views of market failure. Markets sometimes fail because of their design and operating logic. Voluntary exchange by private actors implies that too few of some goods may be produced, too many of some others, and none at all of yet others. If we want to use markets, then we must cope with their failure. In an analogous way, tendencies to failure are inherent in the design and operating logic of bureaucratic systems. Inefficiency or ineffectiveness results from the pursuing of self-interest within a publicly designed set of incentives. As long as we use bureaus, we need to understand their inner propensities for failure from a social perspective.

Chapter 4 discusses the microeconomics of bureaus. It is concerned primarily with their technical and allocative efficiency along with their dynamic efficiency—their incentives and will to innovate. It focuses on their expected levels of output and the social costs of bureaucratic supply rather than their internal politics, except when politics has integral connections to efficiency.[7] It describes and analyzes some of the formal models prominent in modern discussions of bureaucratic resource allocation.[8]

Market Justifications for Bureaus

Given the basic presumption, at least in the United States, that market systems are preferable to other strategies of resource allocation, there are three major justifications for bureaucracies.[9] First, they provide the political, legal, and technical infrastructure that assures that decentralized market systems work well. Given a system of private exchange, they set standards and define the measures that let buyers and sellers know the quality and quantity of the goods and services they may want to exchange. When disputes arise in exchange, they provide means for adjudication of rights and enforcement of contracts. Second, in some cases of market failure bureaucratic supply of goods and services, information or regulation is a legitimate alternative as discussed in chapter 3. Monopoly, public goods, externalities, missing markets, and incomplete information produce market failure. Their presence, however, does not automatically translate into bureaucratic supply.[10] Even if market failure can be clearly identified, this does not by itself tell us that bureaucratic cures or amelioration are feasible and cost-effective.

Among competing forms of intervention, economists prefer and promote those that work through the existing market framework and pricing system. If subsidies or taxes can cure some failure, then either would be a preferred alternative to direct public action programs. These arguments for minimal state activity rest not only on grounds of cost, but also on the qualitative benefits assigned to decentralized market systems. If we want a fast response to changing economic and social conditions, then—the argument goes—indirect, decentralized intervention is necessary to give individuals the freedom to take action without time-absorbing bureaucratic review and consultation.

Third, bureaus modify the income distribution that results from market decisions. Reasonably competitive market systems contain processes and structures that push them toward efficiency. However, they have none that deliver an appropriate distribution of income or wealth. There is no general consensus on distribution, and social and political judgments frequently differ from market judgments. At least in developed economies, there is consensus that those who obtain meager rewards from the operation of the market system must still have some minimum standard of living. In practice, bureaus at many different levels of government work at maintaining a social safety net for those whom the market system has disadvantaged. There is, of course, always fierce debate about the overall size of this net and its design, whether its mesh should be gross or fine.

NATIONAL NEEDS JUSTIFICATIONS FOR BUREAUS

If market failures were the only reason bureaus deliver some goods and services but not others, then in every economy that uses market systems—if not in every economy—we might expect bureaus to produce roughly the same menu of public goods and services. This is not the case, however. In fact, feasible technologies usually exist that will support either public or private delivery. We usually have a choice about delivery strategy. For example, telecommunications and transportation are private goods (but regulated) in the United States and generally public goods in Western Europe. For certain services the United States maintains both public and private delivery systems, for example, in health and education and in the production of gas, water, and electricity.

Furthermore, nations, over time, can find themselves switching between public and private strategies or trying to switch. Here political and ideological factors play a strong role. For example, the Conservative British government has been privatizing the coal industry nationalized by the socialist Labor government in 1948.[11] Then and now there is nothing about coal to suggest that it has standard public good characteristics (nonappropriability and nondepletability) or that domestic and international coal markets make incorrect judgments about the price and quality of British coal. Nationalization, from the perspective of the Labor government, was a way to carry out socialism, not the appropriate treatment for an inefficient natural monopoly. Privatization for Prime Minister Margaret Thatcher is an ideological symbol, not amends for Labor's economic misjudgments about the coal industry. Similarly, Japan has recently switched from public to private telecommunications not because these services suddenly lost their characteristics as public goods, but because of shifts in political perceptions and beliefs about bureaucratic ability to cope with rapidly changing technologies.

The economic judgments made by market systems frequently generate political demands and pressure for intervention, especially when jobs and market share are at stake. Domestic industries facing shifts in demand or rapid technological change insist on government intervention or help. They claim they have special importance for the economy or that their existence provides some desirable qualities in a democratic society.

Industries and firms facing strong foreign competition frequently insist they have a right to have the U.S. government intervene on their behalf in foreign economic affairs. Other governments prevent a "level playing field." For example, in recent years, the government has intervened on behalf of the auto and semiconductor industries. The consumer electronics industry wants the government to set standards and policies for high definition television (HDTV). Otherwise the Japanese will capture the market, for their government has given them a leg up by funding R&D through the publicly owned broadcasting service.

On their side, decision makers often feel impelled to intervene in markets. Many arrive in office because they perceive national needs or public interests unserved by the market.[12] For example, high-quality, affordable day care has become an articulated national need that politicians must address. They or their advisers may believe that markets would continually provide sufficient quality, quantity and variety of day care services. But they may perceive the market as far too slow. The day care market might eventually alleviate excess demand by making more care available. But working mothers are not going to wait for this to happen. In any case, markets are not likely to provide low-income parents with a high quality of day care.

Because judgments about public intervention in markets involve political and bureaucratic issues as well as economic ones, we should expect conflict. Perceptions of national need or of appropriate speed are not the same for all stakeholders. Market failure or success can be defined in different ways, each plausible. Indeed, failure for some is success for others, for actual empirical cases will be ambiguous. If we observe persistent excess demand or supply, we might say the market is moving toward equilibrium but is taking its time, or we might say barriers exist that prevent the market from reaching equilibrium without help. Even if decision makers and stakeholders agree that a market needs help, there will be no agreement over what type. The technical economic situation usually admits a wide range of instruments: for example, tax incentives, public subsidy, public ownership but private operation, or both public operation and ownership. Since the economic situation is rarely decisive, actual outcomes depend mainly on relative power and bargaining capabilities.[13]

SUPPLY PUSH

Independently of the technical character of goods and services and of any perceived national or social needs, there will always be some supply push from existing bureaus to do more for clients and constituents. Given their highly stylized budget process, most bureaus feel impelled to tell sponsors that they are always operating at or just below the critical minimum required to meet their mandated public objectives. They always push for the additional resources they need to operate current programs at a higher level. Requests for the same real level of resources each year would raise doubts about a bureau's competence and motives in the eyes of sponsors. Private firms, it should be noted, also seek to expand, enlarge, and broaden their provision of goods and services. However, the market disciplines them. Public organizations have only the discipline of the electorate and their representatives.

Entirely new programs imply additional staff and budget, these two being among the more important indicators of bureaucratic success. So bureaus push new programs required to perfect their mission. Bureaus that deliver services are always discovering interactions between their own and other services. A common tactic here is to claim that effective service requires grappling with interactions and spillovers. Curing poverty, for example, requires simultaneous programs for housing, education, and health. Thus a welfare agency may acquire innovative education, health, and housing programs—that is, programs that can be substantively and politically differentiated from the mainline programs of single-service housing, education, and health agencies.

Additional programs create multiplier effects. If all service programs are closely linked, they need coordination. For example, representatives of mainline agencies may become advisers to the agency with innovative programs; or the mainline agency may force review or approval of an innovative, competitive program. Similarly, regulatory agencies frequently discover economies of scope and demand greater authority to coordinate. Transportation regulators, for example, frequently have argued that the socially optimal mix can be achieved only if they coordinate or regulate all major modes, even though many of these modes do not have the characteristics of natural monopoly that justify regulation from an economic perspective. For example, the Interstate Commerce Commission until recently regulated most surface transportation regardless of the natural monopoly characteristics of a mode.[14] However, more interaction and coordination creates demand for additional staff and equipment all around.

TOTAL MENU OF PUBLICLY PROVIDED GOODS AND SERVICES

The array of goods and services produced by government thus reflects some combination of (1) perceived market failure and imperfections; (2) political judgments that some goods and services are too important to be left to the market, that their delivery requires central oversight, if not central control; and (3) supply push.

Delivery systems themselves, rather than the particular goods and services they provide, may become a political or a moral issue to be settled in the political arena. For example, the United Kingdom uses voluntary, nonprofit organizations to collect blood, and the United States uses a mixed system of markets and voluntary provision. Some believe that, for some goods, voluntary, nonprofit delivery systems are morally superior to a greed-motivated market.[15] Economists, however, argue that even if public objectives have high moral content, the market will achieve them at the least social cost. Indeed, saving resources via markets is moral because it permits other objectives to be achieved. However, politicians and voters frequently value efficiency less than other properties of an allocation strategy or they have a broader definition of market failure than economists do.[16]

SIMPLE MODELS OF BUDGET ACQUISITION AND OUTPUT

To understand the expected results of bureaucratic resource allocation and compare them with those from market allocation, we can model bureaus as utility or objective maximizers operating under constraints imposed by sponsors and the legal and political environment. This approach retains a rough symmetry with models of private firms and markets. We can then compare optimal outputs and "prices" between the two strategies. As with firms, we want to know (1) how bureaus will behave, and (2) how they ought to behave from a social perspective. We especially want to know how the allocative and technical efficiency of bureaus compares to competitive firms and monopolies if they produced the same outputs and had the same production technologies.

Assume that bureaus offer to produce a certain quantity of output in exchange for budget from a sponsor.[17] The sponsor has a budget evaluation function $B(Q)$ that shows how much it is willing to allocate in exchange for a bureau's promise or offer to produce the quantity Q. The bureau's promise to deliver more Q elicits more budget but at a diminishing rate, hence $B(0) = 0$, $B'(Q) > 0$, $B''(Q) < 0$.

Budget maximization is the traditional starting hypothesis in the economic analysis of bureaus. Assume that bureaus try to maximize $B(Q)$. In federal bureaus the rationale for a budget maximization hypothesis is as follows. The actual performance of federal bureaus is difficult or impossible to observe, so the size of budget and its growth rate become gross indicators of success internally and externally. At the federal level successful administrators are those who obtain larger and larger budgets. Their staffs perceive them as successful, and even sponsors, trained to resist demands for budget, are apt to admire administrators who can maneuver them into providing larger and larger budgets. For example, James Shannon, director of the National Institutes of Health, maneuvered successfully between the president, OMB, and the Congress to obtain increasing budgets throughout the 1950s and 1960s. In contrast, clients and staff both believe that a constant or declining real budget is a visible signal of organizational defeat and decline. Perceived decline leads to actual decline.

Now, simultaneously assume that sponsors insist that any budget must at least cover all costs. The bureau's problem then is to maximize its budget subject to a no-loss constraint, $B(Q) \geq C(Q)$, where C is minimum total cost for each level of Q. $C(Q)$ has standard properties, $C'(Q) > 0$, and $C''(Q) > 0$. In other words, increasing Q increases costs at an increasing rate. The bureau's problem then is:

(4.1)   max $B(Q)$ subject to $B(Q) \geq C(Q)$.

Assuming that the constraint is effective, the bureau's equilibrium output Q^* is given by the solution of

(4.2) $B'(Q) < C'(Q)$

(4.3) $B(Q) = C(Q)$.

At equilibrium, marginal budget is less than marginal cost.[18] But the sponsor's optimal output requires maximizing net benefits $B-C$, leading to the marginal condition $B'=C'$. Since B' is falling and C' is rising, the bureau's optimal output Q^* is greater than the sponsor's optimal output. If sponsors reflect society's desire for Q, then the bureau is allocatively inefficient. It may also be X-inefficient with its actual cost curve lying above the minimum cost one dictated by its production technology.

Figure 9 shows the situation in terms of total budget and cost curves.[19] In the figure, if the break-even constraint is

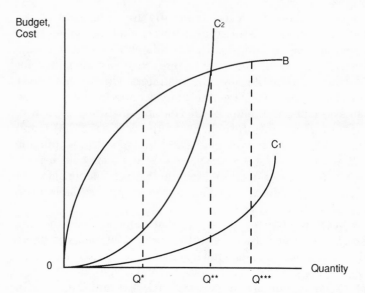

FIGURE 9   *Budget-Maximizing Bureau: Totals*

ineffective, $B(Q)$ reaches its maximum where $B'(Q) = 0$ and $B(Q) > C_1(Q)$. The bureau produces at Q^{***}. At Q^{***}, the bureau is inefficient, both technically and allocatively, relative to Q^*, the socially efficient output. Its output is too large: for that too large output it does not deliver at least cost. At Q^{***}, budget received in excess of cost can be applied to the acquisition of additional inputs, perquisites, or lobbying for more budget in the next cycle. If the constraint is effective, $B(Q) = C_2(Q)$. The bureau wants to climb as far up its sponsor's budget evaluation function as it can, consistently with the break-even constraint. Optimal output for an effective break-even constraint is then Q^{**}. The sponsor's optimum output, however, remains $Q^* < Q^{**} < Q^{***}$, where net benefits are maximized.

Figure 10 shows the same outcomes in terms of average and marginal budget and cost curves. With an ineffective constraint, the bureau sets its output where the sponsor's marginal budget valuation equals zero and average budget

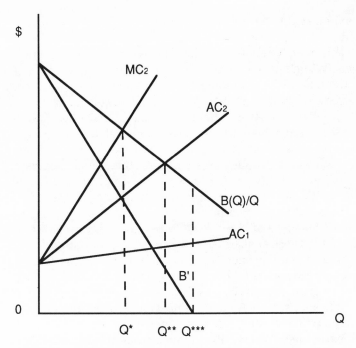

FIGURE 10   Budget Maximizing Bureau (Averages and Marginals)

$B(Q)/Q > AC$. This occurs where the elasticity of the average budget evaluation function, $B(Q)/Q$, is unitary. If the intersection of the average budget line and an average cost line such as AC_2 occurs at elasticities greater than one, then the bureau is cost constrained and produces Q^{**}. Any sponsor interested in maximizing net benefits would, however, desire production at Q^*, as would a perfectly competitive industry faced with a demand curve equivalent of the average budget function.

The power of these results rests on an implicit assumption that a bureau's sponsors cannot apply effective controls to it. The bureau gives sponsors an all-or-nothing choice. Since sponsors themselves are accountable to higher-level sponsors, they prefer some output to no output. It seems that they can do little but acquiesce in the output the budget-maximizing bureau proposes and, thus, to the corresponding budget.

However, sponsors have more power than this model suggests. While bureaus may desire to maximize budget, at least at the federal level, bureaus always exhibit deep fear of—indeed, paranoia about—their sponsors' power. For example, a federal agency gives extraordinary attention to the routine enquiries and demands of its particular legislative and executive sponsors. Even more indicative of its fear is the deference shown to the sponsor's working staff, which exercises far more authority over a bureau than that implied by its place in the sponsor's organization. Agency heads live in fear of the budgetary power of low-level examiners from the Office of Management of Budget (OMB) and congressional staff, especially those concerned with budget appropriations.

Nearly every agency has a congressional liaison branch that coordinates and monitors an agency's interactions with the Congress. Similarly, calls and enquiries from executive branch sponsors—say, the White House or OMB—are answered with extraordinary speed. In fact, the desire to appear or be responsive to executive branch sponsors, especially the White House, provides some explanation of their ability to drag agencies, even against their better judgment, into questionable schemes and activities. Not going along, even on questionable activities, implies that the bureau is not playing on the sponsor's team. Not playing is highly likely to be seen as disloyal and deserving of punishment.[20]

The belief that sponsors lack information about bureaus is also questionable. Sponsors get a continual flow of detailed information from a bureau's clients and constituents. "End runs" by bureau staff are so common at the federal level that some agencies provide written regulations about contacts between staff and sponsors. Employees, however, constantly violate the regulations; indeed, agencies expect them to do so when the end run contributes to some agency purpose. In fact, when an agency wants to send information (or occasionally disinformation) to a sponsor, it may decide to do it via an end run or a deliberate leak. Such methods of transmission may well increase the credibility of a message.

MORE COMPLEX SPONSOR-BUREAU INTERACTIONS

Suppose that the budget-output function can be broken down into a price (demand) component and an output component.[21] For simplicity, suppose that the sponsor has the budget evaluation curve $B(Q) = \alpha Q - \beta Q^2$ and is interested in maximizing net benefits $B(Q) - C(Q)$. It assumes that supply price P is a parameter fixed by the bureau. Total cost is then PQ. So the sponsor maximizes net benefits, $NB = \alpha Q - \beta Q^2 - PQ$. Then the sponsor's demand (willingness to pay) curve is $P = \alpha - 2\beta Q$. If the sponsor reveals this curve to the bureau, then the bureau's problem is maximizing:

$$(4.4) \qquad B(Q) = PQ = (\alpha - 2\beta Q)Q$$

subject to

$$(4.5) \qquad PQ \geq C(Q) = \sigma Q + \delta Q^2$$

$$(4.6) \qquad P = \alpha - 2\beta Q .$$

Then in figure 11 the bureau's optimal output is either $Q^{**} = \alpha - \sigma/2\beta + \delta$, cost constrained case, or $Q^{***} = \alpha/4\beta$. The sponsor's optimum is, however, $Q^* = \alpha - \sigma/2(\beta + \delta) < Q^{**} < Q^{***}$.

If the sponsor does not reveal its demand and asks for the bureau's supply function before making its own decisions, then the efficiency situation improves. The bureau's problem in this situation is to maximize

$$(4.7) \qquad B(Q) = PQ$$

subject to

$$(4.8) \qquad C(Q) = \sigma Q + \delta Q^2 \leq PQ .$$

The bureau has to solve its problem first and convey its solution to the sponsor. From the bureau's perspective, P is given. So its supply price is equal to average cost $P = \sigma + \delta Q$. Now the sponsor maximizes

$$(4.9) \qquad BQ = \alpha Q - \beta Q^2 - PQ$$

subject to

$$(4.10) \qquad P = \sigma + \delta Q .$$

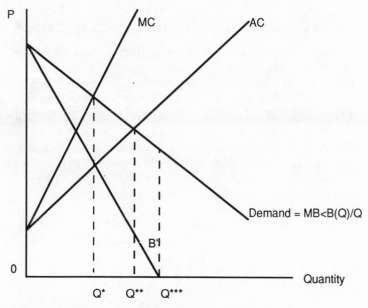

FIGURE 11 *Demand-Revealing Sponsor*

The solution to the sponsor's problem is $Q^* = \alpha - \sigma/2(\beta + \delta)$. It equates its marginal outlay to its marginal benefit. For any given Q the sponsor selects, the break-even constraint forces the bureau to supply at average cost. Thus, in figure 12 the bureau and the sponsor both arrive at the sponsor's optimal output. Relative to the output that would be provided if a competitive industry delivered Q, here the bureau's output is efficient.

THE CASE OF PRIVATE DELIVERY

If one believes that bureaus always overproduce, then a shift in allocative strategy sounds plausible. Sponsors might transfer production to profit-maximizing firms when it is technologically feasible to do so. For a variety of mundane services—sanitation, water, and power—private technology generally does exist. The case for transferring the functions of central government bureaus is somewhat weaker. However, periodi-

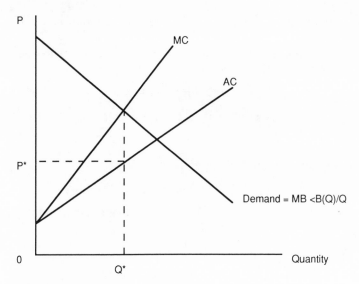

FIGURE 12   *Demand-Concealing Sponsor*

cally federal decision makers insist that the way to achieve efficiency is through contracting out to private vendors.[22]

Suppose a sponsor prefers to contract out the services it funds and that some monopolist is asked to do the job currently done by a bureau. Then the sponsor again faces the issue of whether to be demand revealing or demand concealing. Under either strategy, the private firm does not provide the socially optimal output. In the demand-revealing case, the monopolist maximizes profit

(4.11) $\pi = PQ - (\sigma Q + \delta Q^2)$

subject to the demand revealed by the sponsor

(4.12) $P = \alpha - 2\beta Q$.

This permits the monopolist to set a price P^* where its $MR = MC$. Using the monopolist's optimal P^*, the sponsor then chooses the

$$Q^* = \frac{\alpha - \sigma}{2\,(2\beta + \delta)} \ ,$$

the monopolist's optimal Q^*. But Q^* is less than socially optimal.

Where the sponsor operates in a demand-concealing mode, the monopolist maximizes

(4.13) $$\pi = PQ - (\sigma Q + \delta Q^2)$$

and reports to the sponsor that its supply price is

(4.14) $$P^* = \sigma + 2\delta Q .$$

The sponsor maximizes its net benefit

(4.15) $$NB = PQ - P^*Q = (\alpha Q - BQ^2) - (\sigma + 2\delta Q)Q ,$$

by equating marginal budget valuation to marginal outlay. This gives an optimal output of:

$$\alpha - \sigma/2(\beta + 2\delta)$$

making its optimal output less than the socially optimal one Q^{***}, $\alpha - \sigma/2(\beta + \delta)$. This is shown in figure 13. Thus there is no simple case that converting from public service delivery to a private mode will improve efficiency. Bilateral dealings between public agencies and private monopolies may be no more efficient than those between private bilateral monopolies. The degree of competition among firms that want to deliver public services probably matters a good deal.

COMPLEX INTERACTIONS

In reality, budgets and eventual outputs result from complex, strongly interactive relations between multiple sponsors, bureaus, and clients and constituents. Certainly, the OMB and Congress are no strangers to strategic behavior by federal agencies. Federal agencies have stock strategies that they use to argue for budget increases and to avoid decreases. To obtain additional budget, they allege that they operate below the critical minimum necessary to serve the purposes intended by the sponsor. In the face of budget decreases, they offer to sacrifice the programs most favored by sponsors and clients. For example, in the face of a budget cut under the Reagan administration, the Librarian of Congress closed the

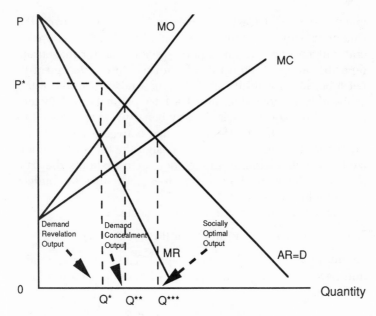

FIGURE 13   *Public Output Using Private Firm*

library at night, which brought about a predictable outcry from patrons and much publicity. In the end, library hours were restored.[23]

While still remaining inside a framework of maximizing objectives, we can build models that take somewhat better account of the interactions. For example, we can give a sponsor the power to punish wayward or lying bureaucracies. The things they value the most can be reduced if they are found out. In such circumstances maximizing bureaus then have to weigh the marginal benefits to be gained from strategic behavior against the marginal costs of being discovered and punished.

Consider the following model:[24] Suppose that a sponsor requires a bureau to reveal the true unit cost P_T of its output. Let the sponsor's demand for output be a function of price, $Q = Q(P)$, $Q'(P) < 0$. Suppose the bureau tries to maximize its expected budget by choosing and reporting a particular estimated price, P_s. Clearly, reported price can differ from the true price. However, any sponsor at all familiar with bureaucratic incentives will anticipate the potential for inaccurate reporting and will equip itself with machinery to detect it. Let θ be the probability of detecting a false P_s and $1-\theta$ the probability of nondetection. If a false estimate is detected, then the sponsor imposes a costly penalty c in proportion to the absolute value of the difference between the reported price and the true price. In this design the bureau is penalized when its estimate undershoots or overshoots the true unit cost. However, the sponsor does not reduce the budget down to the true cost.

The bureau then maximizes its expected budget

(4.16) $E(B) = (1-\theta)B(P_S) + \theta[B(P_T)-c|P_S-P_T|]$

by finding the optimal price to report. The first-order condition for a maximum in the case of a linear demand function $Q = \alpha-\beta P_S$ is:

(4.17) $\partial E(B)/\partial P_S = (1-\theta)(\alpha-2\beta P_S)$
               $-\theta\, c[\text{sign}(P_s-P_T)] = 0$.

This gives

(4.18) $P_S = [\alpha(1-\theta) \pm \theta c]/2(1-\theta)\beta$
               $= \alpha/2\beta \pm \theta c/2\beta(1-\theta)$

The optimal P_S differs depending on the sign of P_s-P_T. This sign depends on the elasticity of the demand curve. Given a linear demand curve, if P_T falls in the elastic part of the demand curve, it will pay the bureau to understate its price, for it can increase its total budget that way. Similarly, if the true price is in the inelastic range, it reports an offer price above its true price. Operating in the inelastic region means that increases in budgets can be obtained by raising the price. Budget is maximized when $P_S = \alpha/2\beta$, when elasticity equals one.

In this model, the two variables under the control of the sponsor are θ, the detection probability, and c, the penalty. The impact of varying these can be determined by comparative statics. If the demand is elastic, then clearly $\partial P_s/\partial\theta > 0$

and $\partial P_s/\partial c > 0$ and vice versa. As θ or c rise, the reported price rises toward the true price in the elastic case and falls toward the true price in the inelastic case. The sponsor in this model thus has two direct policy instruments it can apply to influence the bureau's reporting and its supply function. By devoting additional resources to intelligence, the sponsor can increase its probability of detecting false supply prices. By changing the penalty for lying, it can influence the bureau to bring its reporting into line with actual price.

Such modeling can be carried farther. More complicated demand functions can be used. We can make demand, or θ, or c stochastic. We can make the utility function itself more complex. As is suggested by the literature about the conservatism of bureaus, we can introduce risk aversion into the bureau's calculations by making its expected utility function concave.[25]

Moving outside the model, a sponsor always retains the right and the power to change institutional relationships with its bureaus. For example, Congress recently increased the powers of inspectors general in the line departments in order to increase its detection capabilities. Through organizational or budgetary reform, sponsors can change the shape of the bureau's utility function and its incentives.[26] A sponsor can credibly bluff, and any federal sponsor can certainly make credible threats. As a result, when we allow for strategic interactions between the bureau and its sponsors, simple conclusions about output and efficiency go out the window.

ALTERNATIVES TO OPTIMIZING THEORIES

The models discussed so far are analytic, a priori, optimizing ones that range from the simple to the complex. We derived a bureau's output or supply price by optimizing increasingly complex objective functions with respect to more and more constraints. Sponsors and bureaus, in fact, set budgets and outputs through negotiation and bargaining. Sometimes sponsors engage in coercion. For example, in the 1970s the OMB forced the National Science Foundation to set up an applied research funding program despite the agency's intense dislike of applied research. Lack of compliance by the agency would have had negative effects on the basic research programs the agency strongly preferred.

The objectives of all contending parties, if they have them at all, are very unclear both to themselves and to others. It is hard to know what to maximize. Bureaucrats believe more budget is better than less, but they frequently do not search for a maximum. The case for settling for responsible or satisfying budgets is similar to the one made by advocates for satisficing theories of the firm. First, bureaus cannot truly maximize their budgets, because they do not have technical information about all the possible programs they could operate with the resources they have. They lack political and organizational information as well. Their budget is determined by dimly understood sponsors and clients. At the federal level, these include the administration currently in power, its budget and management agencies, congressional committees, and clients. The processes that sponsors and clients use in forming their views are only partially known to bureaus, and they have no good way of finding out more.

Second, even if bureaus did know the objectives and constraints of all their sponsors, they have only limited cognitive and computational skills for processing that knowledge, and therefore the range of response to a sponsor's decisions will be limited.

Third, the global objectives of bureaus may not be compatible with maximizing budget or utility. To obtain more budget, a bureau may have to accept new programs that are unpalatable or conflict with old ones. Sponsors have their own ideas of the kinds of programs and behavior they want. In some cases, long-run budget maximization might involve stopping current programs with heavy sunk costs. However, stopping programs is a visible confession of failure, and failure will have bad consequences for future budgets. Terminations, no matter how well grounded on cost-effectiveness criteria, raise doubts about a bureau's competence and therefore have a negative impact on prospective budgets.

Given such complexities, one alternative to the standard analytic approach is to simulate the interactions.[27] We can postulate salient events and interactions in the life of a bureau and assign these events some probability. Events that occur or do not occur then affect other events whose probability changes. For example, Bendor and Moe (1985) simulate a three-way interaction among bureaus, politicians, and interest groups. Output and price are the joint outcome of simulated historical events. The bureau responds adaptively to events, and, occasionally, it settles into some price-output equilibrium, which, however, is neither stable nor optimal.

A MARGINALIST PERSPECTIVE: COPING WITH COMPLEXITY

Given the complexity of bureaucratic life, high-profile efforts to maximize budgets may be self-defeating. Administrators may rather aim at significant or sufficient increases over the previous year's budget. In fact, at the federal level they are usually willing to settle for increases of 2–5 percent above inflation. Modest real growth and a low profile may satisfy clients while avoiding intense scrutiny by sponsors and increased demands for cost-effectiveness.

Whatever last year's budget turned out to be represents a generally accepted solution to internal and external constraints and therefore is used as the base for this year's. To this base sponsors will usually add some small percentage increase to allow for normal program growth and, implicitly, for inflation. All parties will send internal and external signals about the acceptability of such an outcome, and bureaus and sponsors strike a deal about overall budget and program composition. Thus the best predictor of a bureau's output is neither the optimal Q^* found by maximizing $B(Q)$ under constraint, nor a new Q^* every year determined by the current year's interactions, but last year's Q.

Incremental or marginal budgeting has tremendous appeal from many vantage points. Essentially it conserves scarce resources of both sponsors and bureaus, and its outcome sends signals to clients and constituents that the situation is normal with respect to the programs they have interests in. In fact, the certainty of modest increases may be more important to bureaus than a large expected increase, although it may be necessary for them symbolically to go through a maximization "rain dance" to please sponsors and clients.

BUDGET ACQUISITION AND PROGRAM IMPLEMENTATION

Once sponsors and a bureau have agreed on a budget and major allocations, they have to be implemented. The bureau has to design programs roughly consistent with its promises and agreements. However, suppose that implementation in fact takes fewer resources than originally estimated. A private firm could and would appropriate the difference as profit. However, unspent funds in a bureau are not profits or additional budget for the bureau: federal bureaus must return unspent funds to the Treasury. In the budget acquisition process, bureaus claim that any budget they receive will be below the optimal amount but that whatever they get will be spent efficiently. Not spending their entire allocation visibly refutes the claims and guarantees they made in negotiating their budget, and this can be costly. Federal agencies that appear to have difficulty spending their budget will receive less in the future, so they have little incentive for operating programs at least actual cost or for cost cutting through learning by doing.

DYNAMIC EFFICIENCY OF BUREAUS

The folklore of bureaus suggests that they are rarely dynamically efficient. Lack of competition, limited search for opportunities around existing programs, and large numbers of constraining laws, regulations, and procedures probably do not make for highly innovative bureaus. However, innovation may be necessary to achieve some of a bureau's objectives. The substance of a bureau's mission may carry within it a demand for new technology, as do the missions of the Defense Department, NASA, and formerly the Office of Economic Opportunity. Furthermore, as bureaus accomplish their missions, budgets and staff stop increasing, or their rate of increase slows. The response may well be a new mission, which may require a new product or new technologies. In fact, some new technologies suggest the feasibility of new missions. For instance, the simultaneous development of seaworthy nuclear power plants and sea-launched ballistic missiles gave the navy a strategic nuclear mission. New technology preferred by an agency may not be cost-effective from a social perspective. Thus, as NASA's budgets fell after the moon shot, it argued strongly for a high-cost, man-in-space technology even though many argued that any space mission that could be done by human beings could be accomplished more cheaply by other means.

Whenever bureaus depend heavily on technology, there will be some technology push. For example, new defense technologies constantly shift advantages from offense to defense and vice versa. The Defense Department seeks to counter the numerically superior forces of the Soviet Union through innovation and technological superiority. There may, however, be a price for the unconstrained pursuit of technological superiority. It may create a bias toward developing systems with high unit costs, thereby reducing the total number of units that can be deployed if development is successful. In heavy combat, large numbers of technologically inferior, cheap weapons can overcome small numbers of superior but expensive ones.

The welfare of particular services and their private-sector defense suppliers also depends on the next generation of technology.[28] Hence each shift in an offense-defense equation produces R&D to offset it. Since technologies are operated by various services—in rivalrous competition—the development of technologies with the potential to shift service budget shares frequently generates offensive R&D by the prospective losers.

No formal models have addressed dynamic efficiency and innovation in bureaus. However, producing socially "correct" behavior over time is as much of problem in bureaus as it is in private firms or more so. Portraits of tired, burned-out, geriatric bureaucracies are staples in the popular literature.[29]

Bureaus seem to pass through a bureaucratic life cycle and climacteric. For example, NASA's climacteric is said to have occurred when it completed the Apollo program in 1969. Once bureaus reach old age, innovation no longer interests them, and their existence becomes a barrier to innovation. At the federal level, decision makers in search of innovation characteristically go around or over their existing bureaus or create new ones. For example, presidents often subvert their own line bureaus when they want innovation. President Kennedy set up the Peace Corps to promote development and kept it out of the Agency for International Development. In waging the War on Poverty, President Johnson felt the need for an innovative agency and therefore set up the Office of Economic Opportunity. President Nixon and Henry Kissinger were notorious for trying to keep innovation in foreign policy out of the hands of the State and Defense departments.

A SIMPLE INNOVATION MODEL FOR A BUREAU

Suppose we analyze bureaucratic innovation through a constrained optimization process. Bureaus have the capability of investing in R&D and now optimize both the quantity of services they want to deliver and their investment in R&D. We want to know whether they would make larger or smaller investments than would be socially optimal.

For simplicity, let R&D be process-oriented and reduce unit costs. Let $c(x)$ be the average cost of output, dependent on R&D, and let x be the costs of R&D. Assume that investing in x reduces c, but at a decreasing rate, $c' < 0$, $c'' > 0$. In the simplest case, the bureau now tries to

(4.19)   max $B(Q)$ subject to

(4.20) $B(Q) - c(x)Q - x \geq 0$.

The first-order conditions for this constrained maximum are:

(4.21) $(1 + \mu) B' - \mu c(x) = 0$,

(4.22) $\mu(c'Q + 1) = 0$, and

(4.23) $B(Q) - c(x)Q - x = 0$.

In the private sector, one standard measure of the intensity of R&D is its ratio to sales. The analogous measure for a bureau would be $x/B(Q)$, the ratio of R&D to total budget. Since there are diminishing marginal returns to R&D cost reduction, then $\mu > 0$, from the required second-order condition, $\mu Q c''(B-c)^2 > 0$. Then $B' > c$. Since $B' > 0$ and $B'' < 0$, the budget-maximizing bureau's output is larger than socially optimal. Marginal budget is less than marginal cost. Now, from (4.22), $dx/dQ = -c'/Qc''$. Since $c' > 0$ and $c'' > 0$, $dx/dQ > 0$. As Q rises, R&D budget rises. Since $d[x/B(Q)]/dQ = [Bdx/dq - xB']/B^2$, and $dx/dQ > 0$, intensity of R&D increases when $dx/dQ/Q > dB/dQ/Q$. Thus, in addition to producing too much, the bureau invests too much in R&D.

Summary

This chapter has explored some simple analytical models of bureaucratic efficiency. Budgets and outputs depend on the sponsor's constraints and information. The models teach us that sponsors with power and sufficient information can make bureaus statically efficient. Making them innovative remains a problem. However, there are some instances where bureaus must innovate, for example, when some innovating rival exists, as in defense. The case literature suggests that innovation requires some internal public entrepreneur and the right environmental conditions. For example, Doig and Hargrove (1988) and Lewis (1980) suggest that innovation in bureaus requires fragmentation of responsibility, constituents or clients demanding innovation, and new technologies to supply the innovation.[30] However, we can easily find cases such as the War on Poverty where public entrepreneurs existed and the environment looked right, but innovation did not lead to "victory." Thus we are a long way from understanding innovation in bureaus.

Chapter 5
Bureaucratic Failure

THIS CHAPTER deals with bureaucratic failure and pathology.[1] Bureaus sometimes fail because of an unusual run of bad luck. They may fail because they face sudden dramatic changes in their environment that no one could foresee even with excellent forecasting and planning. However, the failures of particular interest here are those that are self-generated, those that occur when highly competent administrators and staff run bureaus as they were designed to be run and try to get them to run well. But running them well, as measured by their own internal systems of exchange and reward, does not necessarily lead to achieving social effectiveness or efficiency. In fact, in successful bureaucratic life, many standard efficiency maxims get turned around. For example, efficiency suggests ignoring sunk costs, those already incurred, in resource allocation decisions. A bureau that never worries about sunk costs, however, is a bureau that will soon be in deep trouble. Sunk costs and little discernible product have a strong adverse effect on a bureau's claim to current and future resources.[2]

In market systems, private incentives and organizational structure force firms and entrepreneurs into behaving in certain ways. Analogously, publicly provided incentives and institutions force bureaus and administrators to behave in prescribed or ritual ways. This ritual behavior leads to the public horror stories that afflict all bureaus from time to time.[3] On the inside, however, anything bureaus do always has a well defined logic and rationale. They can prove that however peculiar their actions may seem from a social perspective, well grounded reasons exist inside. In fact, prudent bureaucrats will be careful to lay down a so-called audit trail, which shows how each decision they took was logically and practically dictated by well established, legitimate objectives and procedures.

The forces that control "perverse" behavior by private firms—competition and relatively low entry costs—are not ordinarily present in bureaucratic environments. Some economists advocate head-to-head competition in the delivery of public services, but most sponsors define bureaucratic competition as waste and duplication. Direct command and control serves as substitute for market discipline, but this is not always powerful enough.[4] Control systems are not usually self-adjusting or self-correcting, and a bureau eventually finds ways around them. In fact, every bureau has highly valued "gatekeepers" who hold collective lore about getting around controls in a timely fashion.

The failures that arise from the natural rhythms of bureaucratic life pose highly difficult questions for the design of government. The discussion in this chapter divides failures into static and dynamic ones, retaining symmetry with static and dynamic market failures. Static failures are those in which bureaus are neither efficient nor effective for the missions they try to accomplish. Dynamic failures are those in which a bureau is unable to select the right missions and to innovate. I try to explain the origin of each failure in ongoing, routine operations.

STATIC FAILURES

Rational Limited Search for Alternatives

Standard microeconomic theory posits private decision makers who are fully rational. In the most rigorous sense, this means that they construct complete inventories of all the available and prospective alternatives relevant to their objectives. Further, they have the cognitive and computational ability to compare alternatives to one another against specified levels of performance. They select the alternative that gives the greatest level of performance for a given cost or the least cost for given levels of performance. If they face uncertainty, then they estimate the relevant probability distributions and rates of discount. So they maximize expected performance or rates of return.

There has been a lengthy dispute in microeconomics on how well private sector decision makers fit this rational image.[5] Whatever the case there, few decision makers in the public sector have the necessary capabilities or can exercise them if they do have them. Their knowledge of feasible alternatives is always limited. Technology and market prices do not reveal alternatives; they have to be discovered. But searching for alternatives is costly in resources that can be spared least— time, energy, and attention. So it makes sense to economize on efforts to recognize and define the problem, to limit the range of legitimate alternatives, and to reduce any need to bargain and negotiate with stakeholders. Precedent, standard operating procedures, and audit trails—processes rather than output—thus become critical, for they are the means of economizing on scarce resources. Because it is rational to limit search, bureaus may never recognize socially effective alternatives, and they will usually ignore predictors of trouble about their current alternatives.

Multiple Objectives and Constituencies

Unlike firms, bureaus must be interested in things other than effectiveness and efficiency. At the federal level, for example, the legislation that establishes bureaus usually contains vague and conflicting objectives, because these were necessary to build consensus and get the legislation passed. Congress instructs educational agencies to concentrate on producing cognitive or vocational excellence but also to be certain they do not slight citizenship. It tells scientific research agencies to promote current excellence in science but also to develop breadth and diversity in the research enterprise. It tells regulatory agencies to protect the public interest but also to promote the health of the industry they regulate.

Instructions from sponsors, however, are not the only source of conflicting objectives. Most agencies have constituents or client groups with different interests who, naturally, watch the bureau or that part of it in which they have special interest. Bureaus that do not provide enough services or output soon encounter pressure to do so. But dispensing resources to meet the diverse needs and interests of constituents and clients has no necessary correlation with overall effectiveness. All allocations have to satisfy public scrutiny, with the result that effectiveness comes to mean taking care of constituents or clients. It follows that efficiency means moving resources to them as quickly as possible. Bureaus focus on speeding up the delivery process without increasing the effectiveness of the things delivered.

Permanent Uncertainty About Production Relations

Even if a bureau were aiming at overall social efficiency and effectiveness, there are often no clear tests for them, and stakeholders and sponsors have great difficulty in knowing when they have been achieved. Even if a bureau has good indicators, it has little incentive to send true signals: highly efficient bureaus will not volunteer to absorb fewer resources.

A bureau's production function is only partially known. Inputs and outputs have no fixed technological relation to each other. Outputs depend more on organization than on some identifiable, hard technology.[6] Hence, a bureau never knows exactly what would happen were it to employ alternative combinations of inputs. There is no guarantee that increasing its inputs will increase its outputs; in fact, it is possible to argue that reducing its inputs will increase outputs. Reductions exert pressure to find the relations between input and output.

What a bureau can do in the way of output involves interactions between the quality and quantity of its inputs and its structures and incentives. However, rarely is anyone going to risk experimenting on the bureau to see if the organizational design, the staff incentives, and the production technology can be found that would increase output, let alone maximize it. Rarely will sponsors set up organizations that compete directly. Since knowledge of production relations is always ambiguous to everyone, to survive and prosper bureaus need deliver only sufficient output to client groups. And sufficient output does not have to be provided at least cost. Whether a bureau accomplishes a mission at least cost is not critical inside or outside. No one knows what least cost is, and no bureau is going to be punished by lower profits if it does not minimize costs.

If bureaus faced efficient public competitors, we might be able to gauge their performance by a series of cost-output-effectiveness comparisons. For example, we could compare the performance of publicly owned and operated hospitals, schools, or waste collection agencies with their counterparts in different jurisdictions.[7] Their product lines and clients may be similar, but they often choose different inputs for given budgets. Different inputs would provide clues for pinning down a bureau's production function. We might not be able to identify an entire production function, but we might find some input combinations that were more efficient than current ones.

Private firms could also provide a base for such comparisons if they were efficient and worked in the same line of activity. But it is hard to find such firms. At the local level we can certainly make comparisons of public and private delivery systems for services such as waste collection. There are certainly cities and counties in the United States that illustrate different modes of delivery. However, differences in performance may well derive from differences in objectives rather than superior allocative and technical efficiency. At the federal level it is more difficult to find exemplars. But we can compare, for example, the cost of overnight delivery service between the U.S. Postal Service and private firms, such as Federal Express.

The ways in which bureaus try to differentiate their output can be revealing. For example, air force and navy tactical aircraft are close substitutes in some missions, although both services work hard to show they are not. The revealed preferences of the services and the arguments and data they use to justify their preferences permit some comparisons of efficiency.

Experiments can also be revealing, although it is difficult

to do them well for those big enough to be visible raise questions and doubts about current performance. Sponsors worry about whether they are wasting money on current programs while, in contrast, clients believe in the value of current programs. They see experiments as threats by the very people organized to service their needs. In fact, they have adjusted their behavior to take advantage of current programs.

Displacement of Output Measures by Input Measures

Budget and resource acquisition cycles are always a powerful determinant of the quality of bureaucratic life. With no agreed measures of output, it is easy to equate the public charge of efficiency and effectiveness with the survival and growth of the bureau. The natural tendency inside is to measure performance by the amount of inputs sponsors provide, and consequently bureaus design programs and conspire with their clients and constituents to achieve more staff and budget. It is hard to connect a bureau's social purposes with unique programs. So it chooses to do what it does best, manage inputs such as staff and budget, always assuming that higher levels of inputs yield proportionately higher levels of social output. In fact, without constant efforts to expand inputs, a bureau quickly loses support among its own staff, constituents, and sponsors. Budget is one of the few quantitative measures of performance that everyone can use.

Sponsors, in particular, have no notion of the optimal level of output that their bureaus could achieve if they were truly efficient. More budget, sponsors believe, correlates with more output, if not maximum additional output. They find requests for budget reductions, should anyone ever make them, highly puzzling and suspicious. Such requests immediately raise questions about the competence of the bureau and doubts about its right to future budgets. No one ever believes that a lower budget request results from a bureau's sudden discovery of lower-cost alternatives to deliver the same output.

A request for a reduction becomes an opportunity by a bureau's adversaries to cut its budget further next time round. Furthermore, clients and constituents facing budget restrictions will perceive the bureau as unresponsive. They will bring pressure to bear on the sponsors to embarrass or fire the managers who requested the reductions. Simultaneously, the members of the bureau staff will make end runs around its managers. They will go to sponsors and complain that their bureau is not acting in harmony with its mandate and the clients it was supposed to serve.

Need for Symbols

In addition to their substantive objectives, bureaus have symbolic and signaling objectives. Sponsors and clients need to observe them accomplishing their mission. The administrative sponsor of given bureau is itself a bureau facing conflicting claims and limited resources to meet them. To maintain their sponsors' attention, bureaus have to find visible, timely programs that warrant their budgetary claims. They also need to express sympathy with their clients and be seen to do so.

Programs that satisfy signaling objectives do not necessarily correlate with effective ones. Signals adequate to reassure constituents and to sustain outside pressure for increased budgets may require spreading available resources very thinly. However, effectiveness may require concentration. For example, most of the nation's current scientific output is produced in about fifty to one hundred research universities, and the marginal productivity of additional research dollars sent to them would probably be much higher than dollars sent to lower-rank institutions. But no research funding bureau could pursue such policy for very long. It could devote some resources to raising the capabilities of some of the lower fifty or one hundred, but that would be unacceptable on a larger scale. There is no evidence that bureaus could or would choose a priori those institutions that will be research winners some day. The ultimate allocation, then, is one of fair shares. A research-funding bureau signals that its heart is in the right place, even though everyone knows the small amounts of money it is spreading to all claimants will produce less research output than if it endowed better performers with proportionately greater amounts.

Internal Equity-Effectiveness Trade-offs

There is usually a program trade-off between effectiveness and equity. For the purposes of equity all eligible claimants have to obtain some benefit, even if the overall result is an ineffective program. Even when a program starts out with an apparently effective design with reasonable criteria for eligibility, there will be constant pressure to expand eligibility. Programs that appear inequitable will have great difficulty being implemented at all, much less justifying more resources.

When inequity arises in a market system, those who do not benefit can attribute the outcome to the impersonal market, but they can only with great difficulty bring direct pressure to bear on it. They are certainly free to try changing the market or to regulate it in ways that give redress, but this takes resources, time, and political energy that are not usually available. For perceived inequity in a public program, there is a clear and vulnerable target—the bureau that runs it.

The nominal beneficiaries will protest against inequitable designs and what is more damaging, against the designers and managers. For example, as was pointed out earlier, in the 1960s the Kennedy administration tried to achieve technological breakthroughs in housing construction via differential R&D subsidies. Public R&D funds would have been allocated to some firms rather than others, but the housing industry protested on the grounds of inappropriateness and lack of equity. Resistance to federal industrial policy rests, in part, on its inherent lack of equity. In fact, many believe equity should be a principal objective of all public programs and argue that it should always be a main criterion in the design of any program. Otherwise, society has weak means of promoting equity compared to market promotion of efficiency.

Time Pressure and the Rush to Expend

In delivering goods and services, markets can take a long time to achieve consistency between consumers' and producers' choices. In contrast, bureaus are always short of time to justify the level of resources they receive, for sponsors' budget cycles are usually annual. A bureau's credibility demands that its current budget be expended or, at least, obligated, so there is a constant rush to expend resources. Because future resources depend on using up all of the current budget, bureaus have every incentive to select submarginal projects. However, the submarginality will be difficult to detect, even by bureaus themselves. They are very clever at constructing plausible cases for this or that program or project and at convincing themselves: all possible reasons will be put forward in the hope that at least one, if not all, of them will be convincing.

While the submarginality of programs and projects can always be argued, unexpended or unobligated funds cannot. The latter are clearly visible to all those interested in a bureau, and reflect unfavorably on it and its managers. To appear minimally competent, a bureau must demonstrate its ability to expend all the resources it is given, even if the marginal benefits from its last projects are consistently less than their marginal costs.

The Tenure of Decision Makers and Underinvestment in Long-Run Payoff

High-level managers in the U.S. bureaucracy have short tenure. Unlike managers of firms, public managers retain no ownership claims on their bureau after they leave, and as a result they need not evaluate the effects of their current actions on the future welfare of their bureau. Moving on to a better post depends, at least, on doing no apparent damage during one's tenure, and, at most, on creating some perceived or actual success. Perceived success in the short run—for example, expending budget fast—is far more important than actual success in the long run—getting a problem solved. Solutions usually come long after the tenure of the managers who designed successful programs and set them in motion is over. Decision makers therefore underinvest in programs that will have a long-term payoff.

Reorganizations

All incoming decision makers and administrators want to make short-run marks. To do this they believe they need to bring in people they trust. Because of the power of incumbent staff to negotiate and bargain about their employment status, decision makers and managers come to believe that reorganization is the only way to make personnel changes. Attempts to remove "deadwood" directly bog down in endless negotiations. Managers have to prove that a particular individual has been shirking or has caused measurable damage. Given the highly ambiguous product of most bureaus, such proof is almost never forthcoming, and even when shirking or damage can be proved, the construction of the required paper trail takes a long time.

Reorganization becomes the only alternative. Through clever class actions, particular individuals become targets. For example, suppose that an economist of a certain grade is persona non grata to a new administrator. A reorganization in the name of increased efficiency just happens to make the job of the offending economist redundant. If an employee's job becomes redundant or unnecessary, then he or she can be fired, "riffed," in federal jargon for reduction in work force. However, new managers have little awareness of the rights and entitlements of employees according to civil service or union rules, so that the attempts to change the organization result in a cascade effect. The "deadwood" asserts its seniority and "bumping" rights, and eventually the younger and most technically well-trained staff exit the bureau. Managers end up with a less competent organization, and they incur massive hostility to boot.

History and Sunk Costs

Economic theory holds that all sunk or previously incurred costs should be ignored in current and prospective decisions about projects and programs, since nothing can be done about these. However, bureaus cannot afford to do so because canceling projects whose costs have become excessive earns little credit and reflects unfavorably on the competence and reputation of the bureau. Sponsors provide budget in the first place with the assurance that a bureau can manage its programs and deliver its product on time and within estimated costs. Cancellations, however rational from an efficiency perspective, mean that there will be no visible result of past expenditures.

Such an outcome will be politically and organizationally unacceptable. Completion of a program or project is far preferable, even when its expected benefits are known to be less than costs and the expected costs are high in absolute magnitude. In the development of a supersonic civilian aircraft, for instance, the British and French completed the Concorde, knowing that the plane would have great difficulty in ever breaking even. The United States only with great difficulty and inordinate cost stopped work on its Clinch River breeder reactor.

Sunk costs in themselves often justify an effort to continue. Large sunk costs and zero output or unfinished programs create perceptions of incompetence that managers seek desperately to avoid. Completing projects or programs with large sunk costs can always be justified by claiming that critics have underestimated the benefit side. Original benefit estimates may not have included the learning that has occurred or the unexpected positive spillovers to other economic sectors. For example, NASA's shuttle program, when fully operational, may attract customers not included in the original benefit-cost computation.

The vulnerabilities created by acting as if sunk costs do not matter are so great that it is only with extreme difficulty that bureaus or governments extricate themselves from unfavorable situations. In fact, when agencies receive genuine signals of difficulty or failure, they read and interpret them as signals of near success. Success requires only a little more effort. In firms managers who recommend canceling a program and allocating resources to an activity or program with higher payoff frequently receive greater responsibility. In bureaus this rarely happens. Managers who suggest stopping an ongoing program are not on the team and will not prosper.

Crisis Management

When some control system breaks down, decision makers and administrators go into a crisis mode, redesigning their systems to be able to handle the problem of the moment and any future ones like it. But as the sense of crisis fades, bureaus see the new system as an impediment to sensible operations, and competent staff seek ways to get around it or sabotage it in the good cause of efficiency and effectiveness. As the staff subverts successive control systems, anomalies and errors begin to creep back in until another horror story triggers renewed efforts at control.

Double Moral Hazard

A form of double moral hazard is involved in attempts to control bureaus directly. Sponsors attempts at control or regulation provoke imaginative attempts to subvert controls, and subversion produces additional efforts at control or attempts to get jobs done by other means. For example, proposed budget cuts generate intensive efforts to get around them. A bureau's incentives to find new lines of work increases, and it may discover and mobilize previously unserved constituents who exercise their legitimate "rights" to public resources. Consequently budgets sometimes rise in response to proposed cuts. Similarly, the imposition of personnel ceilings or cuts generates an intensive search to get around them. For example, if there is a lid on permanent civil service staff, there may be none on temporary staff, so full time equivalent staff expands.

Once sponsors observe some adverse response, they modify their original rules: instead of putting ceilings on the number of permanent staff, they now place a limit on fulltime equivalent staff. In response a bureau contracts out work that staff are doing, thereby raising its expenditures. Observing the rise, sponsors set rules and limits on direct expenditures. But there may be no limit on interagency transfers of resources, and so a bureau offers to work for another on contract.

Given such interactions, sponsors' costs of control start going up. Bureaus with multiple sponsors involved in complex contractual relations need coordination, and consequently sponsors need more resources and staff. Thus they now suffer from moral hazard and must play the same games with the higher level sponsors to whom they report. The final outcome is a more complex, costly, and unresponsive bureaucracy, a state of affairs that no one intended.

DYNAMIC FAILURES OF BUREAUS

In the discussion of firms in chapter 2, we noted that, other things being equal, market forces tend to make them statically efficient. However, we noted that, while static efficiency is desirable, even greater welfare gains come from dynamic efficiency. In the private sector, there is a continuous process of invention, innovation and diffusion.

Bureaus, of course, have opportunities for innovation just as firms do. Significant potential for process economies can be found in all bureaus, given their intense involvement in the production and transmission of information and entitlements using paper media. The electronic media can be a highly cost-effective substitute for paper media. The last three federal administrations, for example, have all tried to apply new computer technology to information handling in the Social Security Administration. At state and local levels, both product and process innovations are frequently possible; for example, solid waste recycling technology increases the cost-effectiveness of collection efforts. We need to ask whether bureaus encounter barriers to innovation analogous to the ones that exist in firms. Some common barriers are listed below.

Myopia About the Future

The bounded rationality in bureaus, the intense time pressure, the cycle of highly prescribed daily activity, and the belief that any surviving bureau must already have discovered efficient and effective alternatives all mean that they focus on today's problems and alternatives. Systematic search for new technologies is not common, even though many bureaus contain R&D branches for exactly this purpose. Policy making or operating branches seldom use information produced by the R&D branches or they use it selectively.

At the federal level innovation usually requires some external crisis or singular event that threatens a bureau's welfare. Sponsors may unexpectedly impose new demands that require innovation—say, a moon shot, a war on poverty, or a general environmental cleanup. A sudden increase in external political demand for innovation catches most bureaus short of viable alternatives, especially when the new demand stems from significant change or perceived crisis in the external operating environment.

There is little internal flexibility or time to do serious planning and analysis in a crisis. A bureau may try searching for new alternatives, but it will probably be too late, and the only programs available will be scaled-up versions of current ones or initiatives that sponsors have previously rejected. Hence a serious crisis or a significant change in environment means that sponsors have no choice but to accept previously rejected proposals. They need to be seen to be doing something, but they have usually exerted no prior demands for contingency planning. There is no assurance, of course, that these old alternatives satisfy new social demands or are consistent with a transformed environment.

Seeing the lack of effective alternatives, sponsors come to believe that their traditional bureaus are incapable of overcoming their parochial interests and producing "imaginative" solutions, and so they set up emergency task forces and crisis management teams at highly centralized levels to work on the problem. They exclude the bureaus with program responsibilities. However, excluded bureaus still have to implement the centrally produced solutions, and once excluded, they have little incentive to implement the new solution imposed by their sponsor either fast or well.

Biases in Type of Innovation

A bureau's output depends on interactions between its inputs and its organizational design, hence innovation usually changes factor proportions in unfamiliar and surprising ways. Innovation probably requires factor proportions that no one has tried and experienced.

In the United States, the response to this problem of factor proportions is bimodal. Where programs are highly equipment-intensive, bureaus prefer innovations that are complex, sophisticated, expensive, and of high quality. Where programs are highly labor-intensive, they prefer innovations that are labor-intensive. Hard technology is rarely seen as a substitute for labor in bureaus that provide services because they believe important tacit knowledge cannot be embodied in equipment.

This bimodal bias is easy to explain, since it contributes to increasing budget for both technology-oriented and service-oriented bureaus. However, if bureaus only use ever higher-quality equipment to substitute for the equipment they have and more labor for labor-intensive activities, overall capability will eventually fall. In practice, the higher the "hard" technology embodied in public goods, the more costly they will be. At some point, quantity-quality trade-offs may become unfavorable. If service improvements can be achieved only with higher quality, better trained staff, ceilings on cost and numbers will be encountered. Some cost-effective hard technologies will be overlooked.

Lack of Evaluation

Unless a bureau has the capability of evaluating and stopping ongoing programs, its ability to innovate is limited. The level of resources "required" or demanded by constituents and clients always rises to the level of resources received. To innovate, bureaus must acquire new resources, but each succeeding increment is harder and harder to get. Alternatively, they must free up current resources, but bureaus are understandably biased against evaluating their programs and using the information to reallocate. Although in theory it can lead to increased budgets, evaluation is inherently critical, and the criticism can be used to reduce budgets. Bureaus are far more sensitive to downward than to upward fluctuations in budget. Decision makers and administrators who embark on serious evaluations may become, unwittingly, the most dangerous adversaries of their own programs. To obtain resources, they have to be unswerving, loyal advocates of their ongoing programs. Evaluation casts doubt on current programs and produces information that a bureau's adversaries can use.

A DOCTRINE OF SUFFICIENCY

There are political and organizational criteria that have to be satisfied in order for any bureau to be run successfully. The visible hands of decision makers, legislators, constituents, and clients propel bureaus into behavior that is internally rational and logical. Some of this behavior seems counterproductive from an "objective" social perspective; for instance, with less "waste," some people could be made better off. However, waste from a bureau's perspective can be a necessary transaction cost, and if sponsors eliminated it, the bureau would probably function less well or not all. Given all the impediments to effectiveness and efficiency, and given the organizational and personal requirements for making bureaus grow and prosper with respect to budget, staff, and other inputs, managers may justifiably reason that their overall purposes will be better served without striving for maximal efficiency. Providing sufficient levels of effectiveness and efficiency over a long time may be highly reasonable, even though it wastes some social resources.

AN APPRAISAL OF BUREAUCRATIC STRATEGIES

Suppose policy designers suggest using a bureaucratic strategy to solve a problem. We apply the appraisal factors of chapter 2. The great virtue of bureaus is that they can concentrate resources on well-identified problems in a timely fashion. NASA, in its work on the 1961–69 Apollo project, and the navy, in its work on the Polaris missile system, are famous examples of bureaus able to do this in the past.[8] However, there have been questions about their ability to do this now: for instance, in NASA's shuttle program, and the navy's carrier programs.[9]

Solving problems effectively in a short time implies that bureaus are not likely to be efficient. When we want solutions fast, we may tell an agency to try everything now, even when we know that we could gain greater technical or allocative efficiency if we allowed a longer time for development of especially promising programs. If we want efficiency along with speed, then we may have to provide special incentives or add additional layers of control.

Bureaus may or may not be dynamically efficient depending on the behavior of their internal and external rivals. However, innovating bureaus will meet difficulty over time: sponsors' commitments to innovation fall as it is achieved and becomes part of routine; and rivals argue that they can carry out now proven, standardized programs better and more efficiently than the innovator. The Office of Economic Opportunity, for example, started as the innovating bureau in the poverty field, but its antipoverty missions ended up inside mainline departments.[10] The office itself eventually disappeared, some of it absorbed into the Department of Health and Human Services.

Compared to problem solving via incentives and markets, bureaus are highly visible. In fact, it is sometimes in the interests of sponsors and clients to make them visible. At least in the short run, it may be politically prudent to set up a new, highly visible bureaucracy to solve a problem or else to give existing ones a highly public assignment. Stakeholders will then concentrate their attention on getting their fair share from the visible bureau. Their demands for equity come to rest on the bureau with the assignment, not the sponsor.

From one perspective, it would seem that bureaus are more corrigible than markets. Managers can give direct orders and check on how they were carried out, and although most managers are limited in the punishments and rewards they can bestow, they do have some at their disposal. However, the corrigibility and controllability of bureaus must be rated as problematic. Over time, any competent bureau learns its way around controls set up by its managers and sponsors: getting its principal jobs done justifies getting around rules and control. As a result, there is a constant battle to maintain control, which higher management rarely wins in the long run. It may be achieved in the short run. For example, management can install some new budgeting language such as zero base budgeting or some new management language like MBO. Bureau staff and stakeholders will initially be unfamiliar with their syntax and meanings. They can be used to reveal preferences and change allocations. But all such languages lose their power eventually.[11] Bureau staff and stakeholders eventually learn to handle whatever language of control sponsors like. Since bureaus overcome all reforms in the long run, there will be a steady stream of reform movements on the outside. As each wave of reform is installed and assimilated, conditions become ripe for the next wave.

Chapter 6
Regulation

IF MARKET SYSTEMS need to be preserved but there are public interests not expressed or inadequately expressed in them, then regulation is a halfway house between markets and bureaucratic provision of goods and services. Regulation constrains the behavior of firms or entire industries, but it preserves market frameworks and private transactions. By imposing profit or operating constraints on firms and industries, regulators try to make private decisions lead to reasonable social outcomes, that is, the outcomes that would have resulted if the public interest could be expressed in markets.

This chapter (1) sketches the general background and rationale for both economic and social regulation, (2) explains how regulation works, and (3) appraises it as a problem-solving mechanism, as we earlier appraised markets and bureaus.[1] The focus is strategic—how to think about regulation as a policy instrument competing against other instruments—rather than tactical—advocacy of particular pricing schemes for public utilities or design of markets to achieve environmental or health standards.

HISTORICAL DEVELOPMENT

Government regulation of economic activity was the norm, not the exception, perhaps to the time of Adam Smith. There was little that might be called coherent national economic policy or central planning as we understand these concepts today. However, the state, at least in Western Europe, occupied itself with the micromanagement of economic affairs. It designed and implemented targeted industrial policies. It licensed guilds and crafts; granted monopolies and subsidies to industries and enterprises it believed furthered its political purposes; and imposed restraints on domestic and international trade. The best economic theory of the day defined adequate performance as self-sufficiency in producing goods and services and maintenance of a permanently favorable balance of trade. Trading systems that were well regulated by the state were believed necessary to achieve these objectives. Few before Adam Smith believed that a nation's wealth consisted of its productive capacity and that a self-regulated economic system could maximize this capacity.

As unregulated market systems spread, there were significant increases in productivity, growth, and welfare. But market adjustments usually hurt some individuals and groups. They took their grievances into the political arena, demanding that the state control or regulate the new industrial system. Preferred means of control differed from nation to nation depending on history and experience. Countries in Western Europe usually opted for state ownership, at least of major natural monopolies, whereas in the United States fair rate-of-return regulation and antitrust legislation became the preferred mechanisms.[2]

Besides responding to political pressures to regulate markets, the state frequently helped develop some industries because they were strongly connected to political, economic, and security interests. However well private markets might work, they would not ordinarily account for political needs to bolster state power or improve military capability. For example, heavy government involvement in the development of railroads was common in both Europe and the United States. After the Meiji restoration in 1868, the Japanese state took a strong role in developing industry and creating markets and comparative advantage. As a late starter in the economic development race, Japan never viewed a minimalist state as advantageous.[3]

THE SCOPE OF REGULATION IN THE UNITED STATES

By the beginning of the twentieth century, the United States had some experience with both economic and social regulation. Congress established the Interstate Commerce Commission in 1887 and passed the Sherman Antitrust Act in 1890. It passed the Food and Drug Act in 1906 to ensure safe foods and medicines. In a country that believed in the superiority of markets for resource allocation, the act emphasized more information for consumers by requiring medicines to have content labels; foods and drugs that contained substances known to be unsafe for human use were banned. Parallel with stepped-up federal efforts, several states established health and safety regulations covering the workplace.

Nevertheless, up to the time of the New Deal, federal involvement in both economic and social regulation remained modest. New Deal programs aimed at large-scale reform and regulation of the market system. The attempt to form cartels of major industries under the National Industrial Recovery Act was declared unconstitutional.[4] But by 1940 the communications, housing, securities, banking, and energy markets were all subject to some federal regulation, and enough New Deal programs and agencies existed to challenge the idea that government's only legitimate role was maintaining the infrastructure required for efficient private markets.

World War II further legitimized regulation. Regulation and central allocation of inputs and outputs are the essence of a wartime economy. Certainly, giving the federal government formal responsibility right after the war for maintaining full employment implied acceptance of some macroeconomic regulation. Yet regulation did not expand much until the 1960s and early 1970s when citizens and decision makers became aware that the United States faced large-scale, potentially irreversible environmental damage. As a result, the federal government acquired greatly enlarged powers to regulate any economic activity that impinged on the environment.[5]

At the same time, major questions were raised about whether industry was sufficiently motivated and active in maintaining the health of workers and the safety of consumers. Industry's perceived indifference to certain social costs of production led to formation of new kinds of regulatory agencies that had power over the operations of entire industries— for example, the Environmental Protection Agency (EPA), Occupational Safety and Health Administration (OSHA), and Consumer Product Safety Commission (CPSC).[6]

In the 1970–80 period, the U.S. economy simultaneously suffered from high inflation rates, low growth of output, and slow growth of productivity. Regulation was not the sole or even the most important factor contributing to these conditions. For example, environmental regulation reduced productivity growth by .4 percentage points in the 1970s.[7] However, many feared that the combined impact of all the new and old regulation was reducing economic performance and expressed fear that regulation had damaged the economy's ability to grow rapidly. Certainly, no one had ever estimated the joint effects of all the economic and social regulation now on the books. Regulation had been imposed piecemeal to address pressing political issues or crises created by newly emerging interest groups, each of whom spoke for a particular cause or problem.

By the mid-1980s, a deregulation movement had gained strength. The federal government eased up on economic regulation of civilian aviation, trucking, and telecommunications. Regulators and legislators, backed up by economists, considered many other industries as ripe for the same treatment.[8] Democratic and Republican presidents alike tried to get the regulatory agencies to think through their indirect impacts as well as direct ones. Beginning with President Ford, agencies proposing new regulation were required to send to the OMB benefit-cost estimates of both direct and indirect impacts. Everyone knew such estimates would inevitably be flawed, indeterminate, and biased. However, the central regulatory review focused bureaucratic attention on overall social outcomes, or at least outcomes of interest to the incumbent administration, rather than the things of immediate interest to the regulatory agency and its clients. Furthermore, review procedures were themselves a means by which the president could regulate nominally independent regulatory agencies. OMB slowed the flow of regulations by forcing agencies to construct and defend their estimates.

THEORIES OF REGULATION: EXPLAINING EXISTENCE

Several major theories have been advanced to explain the existence of regulation. The public interest theory is the oldest. Today it competes with a variety of "capture" theories. Each theory has political correlates and carries with it an implicit or explicit action program.[9]

Public Interest Theories

In public interest theories, the state undertakes regulation because it has received true signals that some politically or socially important market or industry is failing. The state undertakes regulation to make outcomes in the failing market come closer to public interest outcomes. However, public interest outcomes may bear no relation at all to economically efficient ones.

The public interest concept extends well beyond any need to correct market failure. Market "success" in the form of high prices and profits may trigger demands for regulation. The public may well believe that the prices an industry charges discriminate against consumers or other important economic classes, or that producers deliberately act against an identifiable public interest. Government aggregates from all sources the public interest demand for regulation and then supplies it. Public interest theory assumes that regulatory bureaus are competent or else can be made so by suitable reform. It also assumes they will have no difficulty designing and implementing regulation consistent with the public interest now and in the future.

The corollary political action program is (1) to promote regulation wherever markets do not provide correct public interest outcomes and (2) to make existing regulation as effective, responsive, and timely as possible.

Capture Theories

Here the demand for regulation, directly or indirectly, comes from the firms and industries facing regulation.[10] Firms receive significant benefits from regulation, since, at heart, regulation is a technique for reducing competition and achieving monopoly rents. Whatever rhetoric may be used as a public justification, regulation actually shelters firms from potential rivals and from application of antitrust constraints. Regulatory agencies—and the public they nominally represent—assume the costs that firms desiring monopoly power would incur in policing their industry to prevent the emergence of rivals. Once an appropriate regulatory structure has been designed and set up, the political program of any regulated industry is, of course, to maintain the status quo in the face of economic and technological change.

In capture theories, the state supplies just the right kind of regulation. Producers have sufficient political and economic power to bring to bear on legislators and administrators. How they acquire this power and overcome other groups with power—including public interest groups—is unspecified.

Bureaucratic Theories

In bureaucratic theories, regulation is the natural result of bureaus seeking to enlarge their turf. The more areas and functions they regulate, and the higher the frequency of their enforcement actions, the more they can acquire the measures of bureaucratic success. Here regulation is a supply-push phenomenon, with bureaus trying, more or less honestly, to convince clients and constituents that expanded rules and regulations are in their own best interests, or, at least, serve to protect them from bad outcomes.

Life Cycle or Evolutionary Theories

These theories combine elements of the previous three. They argue that agencies begin with a vigorous public interest perspective and age progressively. In old age they come to favor the regulated industry. At some point, the inefficiencies induced by regulation become sufficiently noticeable to the public that calls for reform or deregulation arise, and a new cycle begins.

EXISTENCE THEORIES AND POLITICAL PROGRAMS

Belief in some particular existence theory conditions the political programs that stakeholders want to pursue. If the capture theory truly describes the situation in regulatory agencies, then, from the perspective of public interest theory, important jobs of regulatory reform and housecleaning need to be done. Public interest advocates want to make captured agencies cost-effective again by streamlining procedures and information flow. They believe there are good people out there who can make a difference. If public interest executives replace "tainted" executives, then captured agencies can be returned to their public interest roots.

From the perspective of industries that have captured a bureau, the political job is to maintain the flow of benefits. As technologies change, the captors seek to slow down their diffusion. As changing market structures permit entry, captors want their agencies to impose entry barriers. Thus, captured agencies generate more and more regulation.

If one believes that regulation is a supply-push, bureaucratic phenomenon, then the first priority is to deregulate. If deregulation is infeasible, then one can always slow a regulator down with requests for cost-benefit or risk-benefit analysis. Furthermore, political sponsors can reduce the supply push by reducing budgets and staff or refusing to fill appointments.[11] And sponsors can always appoint senior managers who oppose a regulatory bureau's activities.

From the standpoint of welfare economics, the job is to deregulate all industries that do not have natural monopoly characteristics. For those that do, some form of constrained pricing (Ramsey) should be used wherever it is politically feasible.[12] If such pricing is infeasible, then thresholds of enforcement should be raised. Higher thresholds of enforcement are a form of deregulation.

Countercapture

In recent years, a theory of "countercapture" has emerged. Groups with strong beliefs in the value of social regulation capture many of the agencies. Their political program is to enforce regulation strictly, not worrying much about its overall cost-effectiveness or negative spillovers. Perceived behavior of such social regulators in the Carter administration led the Reagan administration to impose additional layers of regulatory review. OMB review forced the agencies to compute the expected, indirect impacts on productivity, inflation, and innovation, although such impacts were not usually part of the regulatory mandate.[13]

SOUNDNESS OF REGULATION THEORIES

None of the various regulation theories by themselves or collectively have much explanatory power. We can talk, metaphorically, about the demand and supply of regulation in some political arena, but this does not explain how competing demands for regulation arise and what the outcomes will be. Certainly not all regulation can be explained by capture. Industries do not always, or even usually, rush to be regulated—especially when regulation concerns cost-increasing health or safety measures. Furthermore, the pressures on bureaucrats and legislators from aroused public interest groups can be as strong as or stronger than those exerted by industries desiring regulation.

Theories that explain the existence of regulation do not help explain the kinds of regulations that agencies will promote. Regulatory agencies have very wide latitude to set rules and standards. The internal organizational requirements of agencies will have a strong effect on the design of rules and standards, irrespective of the group that has captured the agency. In any case, rules and standards are always subject to legal challenge and judicial evaluation, and regulatory agencies and their captors both know this. Regulators are not automatically free to confer benefits on their captors. Such benefits, on their face, have to be related to an agency's formal regulatory mission. An agency must be prepared to show how benefits were justified in suits brought by disgruntled stakeholders or public interest groups.

Given the very wide range of regulation in the United States, a public interest explanation may be appropriate in some contexts, a capture theory in others, and a bureaucratic theory in yet others. Regulation probably has been imposed on pragmatic grounds, without reference to any a priori theories of regulation. Decision makers and politicians simply see regulation as the quickest and most visible solution to a problem or crisis. Similarly, interest groups and stakeholders who want to solve a problem or resolve a crisis find that direct regulation may be the easiest, if not the most cost-effective, way to do so. Bargaining about using marketlike mechanisms can easily be interpreted as a sellout, and this will dilute the power of interest groups.

While decision makers might be able to design relatively pure market regimes to handle problems, these have significant disadvantages from a political and organizational view (chapter 3). Hence the natural response of legislators and administrators is to put regulations on the books and not to worry too much about their efficiency or effectiveness. The act of regulating can be accomplished quickly and visibly; in the short run, any lack of effectiveness or efficiency will not be particularly visible, and the short run is of most concern. Thus the regulatory regimes we observe probably reflect routine exercises in legislative and bureaucratic rationality rather than clear expressions of the public interest or the tacit collusion of legislators and administrators with their captors.

Such a view is bolstered by changes in the perception of regulation. Until recently, in itself it was not an important category of decision. Government did not try to determine, ex ante, the aggregate amount of regulation it would supply, nor were there attempts to measure the government's regulatory expenditures or impacts. Each regulatory agency has different reasons for its existence and its behavior, reasons that have less to do with general theories of regulation than with the political and economic environment in specific industries.

THEORIES OF DEREGULATION

Robust regulatory theories should be able to explain transitions from regulated to deregulated states and vice versa. The theories of regulation do not explain the wave of deregulation in the United States in the late 1970s and 1980s. One can argue that new technology puts pressure on some regulated industries such as telecommunications, but regulators have been able to control applications of new technology in the past. One can argue that regulation over a long time creates a set of disgruntled stakeholders, who then collude with consumers fed up with inefficiency and high prices, and increase pressures on administrators and legislators. One can argue that the economists' invention of contestability theory undercuts the standard rationale for regulating a significant number of industries as natural monopolies, particularly the airline industry.[14] But none of these arguments makes a coherent theory of deregulation.[15]

ECONOMIC REGULATION:
THE CASE OF NATURAL MONOPOLY

Figure 14 presents the standard portrait of a natural monopolist. Monopoly is said to be natural when the total cost of supplying a market at all possible levels of output is less than the total cost of two or more firms supplying the same market. A more familiar way to define single-product natural monopolies is in terms of their average and marginal cost curves. Natural monopolies are firms that can achieve economies of scale, that is, continuously declining average and marginal cost curves up to the entire size of the market.[16]

Such curves arise in industries characterized by very high ratios of fixed to variable costs, hence the traditional identification of natural monopoly with "networked" industries, in particular, public utilities. To operate at all, firms must incur high costs setting up networks and facilities to transmit the product. Once the network has been set up, the variable costs of transmission are very low, so that the larger the firm's scale of operations, the lower its average and marginal costs become. If several firms initially have the same cost structures, then they are in a race to see who can operate at largest scale and capture the entire market.

The pricing rules for any profit-maximizing monopolist are: (1) produce that quantity where marginal revenue equals marginal cost; and (2) set price equal to average revenue. Thus the unregulated monopolist in figure 14 chooses the output Q_M and price P_M. The application of these rules results in allocative inefficiency—the firm does not produce enough, and its price is too high relative to a perfectly competitive market structure.[17] The monopolist's privately optimizing behavior results in an overall "deadweight loss," shown by the shaded area of figure 14.

THREE MECHANISMS

Besides living with this allocative inefficiency,[18] there are three alternative mechanisms for controlling natural monopoly in the United States—(1) application of the antitrust

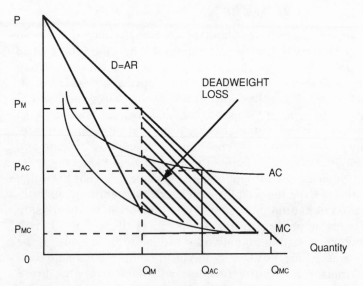

FIGURE 14   *Single Product Natural Monopoly*

laws to break up the monopoly, (2) public ownership, and (3) regulation.[19] The antitrust cure may be worse than the original problem. Making smaller firms out of a natural monopoly will not necessarily result in lower prices: the inefficiency of smaller firms under natural monopoly conditions implies that to earn a normal return, they will have to charge a price, which could easily be higher than the profit-maximizing price the monopolist would charge if left alone. Furthermore, the transactions costs associated with modern antitrust cases are very large. Even if antitrust were an appropriate policy, it takes a very long time to work itself out.[20]

Public ownership raises directly all the issues concerned with bureaucratic rationality already discussed. There is no guarantee that publicly owned firms would pursue allocative and technical efficiency even if their sponsors made them prime objectives. Publicly owned firms can easily be high-cost firms, since cost minimization is not usually consistent with meeting bureaucratic objectives.[21]

Sponsors can, of course, use internal regulation. For example, publicly owned firms that consistently lose money may face a break-even constraint. Where a private market exists for the output of some publicly owned firm, sponsors can instruct the firm to maximize consumers' surplus or some other welfare criterion subject to some break-even constraint, the result of which will be a set of constrained marginal cost-pricing rules that public firms will be expected to follow.

A break-even constraint makes subsidies from general revenue unnecessary if the public firm manages to satisfy the constraint. However, such a constraint has to be made operational by setting up standard pricing rules and procedures, and their design can easily drift away from sponsors' intents and constraints. Publicly owned firms will not go out of business even if they fail to satisfy break-even constraints or other internal requirements.

The poor performance of public enterprises has led many decision makers to conclude that privatization of public enterprises is the only way to get them to take efficiency and competitiveness seriously.[22] However, we saw that privatization does not necessarily lead to an optimum from the perspective of sponsors or the public.

The main argument for regulation is that, at least in principle, it achieves most of the social gains that can be reaped from the other two alternatives. Compared to antitrust action, regulation does not require setting up whole new market structures. Compared to public ownership, it retains some efficiency incentives—unless, of course, regulators unknowingly impose rules that provide incentives for inefficiency. For example, in figure 14, the regulator might try to set prices at the break-even point, P_{AC}. P_{AC} is not the most efficient outcome but price is lower and quantity greater than that provided by an unconstrained monopoly.

THEORY OF RATE-OF-RETURN REGULATION

The regulator picks a fair rate of return which the firm is expected to meet. On the input side, the firm's problem is max profit:

$$(6.1) \qquad \pi = P(Q)Q - rk - wL$$

subject to the production function:

$$Q = F(K,L)$$

the regulatory constraint,

$$(PQ - wL)/K \le s > r$$

and,

$$K, L > 0,$$

where K and L are capital and labor, r and w are their respective costs, and s is the allowed rate of return.

Then the constrained marginal rate of substitution is:

$$(6.2) \qquad -dL/dK = r/w - \mu (s-r)/(1-\mu)w.$$

Since μ can be shown to lie between 0 and 1, it follows that:

$$(6.3) \qquad -dL/dK < r/w .$$

This means that the regulated firm will not minimize cost for the output it chooses to produce. Cost minimization requires that the marginal rate of technical substitution equal r/w. Given the convex nature of production isoquants, rate-of-return regulation implies that the firm uses more capital and less labor than it would have if it were minimizing cost. This can be shown in figure 15.

In figure 15 we fix output at some arbitrary Q. The profit-maximizing firm wants to produce at least cost for any Q. The desired output is shown by the isoquants Q_1 and Q_2. Then to satisfy the constraint and be on the isoquant Q_1 the firm has to produce at point E', not the least-cost point E. But point E' uses more capital K^{**} than point E, where K^* is used. As desired Q changes, the least-cost path lies below the constrained path until they meet at a point where output is so large the constraint is no longer effective.

One of the original justifications for regulation was that it would increase allocative efficiency by forcing monopolists to offer more output than they ordinarily would. If a larger

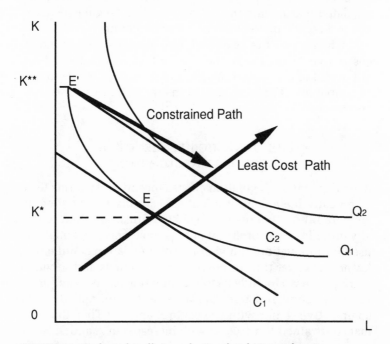

FIGURE 15   *Technical Inefficiency by Regulated Monopolist*

output were always the result of rate-of-return regulation, then induced decreases in technical efficiency could be balanced against increases in allocative efficiency. Regulators could seek a rate of return that just balanced the marginal benefits of increased output against the marginal costs of decreased efficiency.

Increases in output are not, however, universally the result of regulation. The firm will use greater amounts of capital as the allowed rate of return falls toward the market cost of capital r, but the amount of labor the firm chooses to use will not necessarily increase. So output need not be larger. However, firms with homogeneous production functions will produce greater output. From the firm's perspective, it operates on an apparently lower marginal cost curve, since the effect of regulation is to lower the marginal cost of capital. Given two firms with identical positive, homogeneous production functions, one regulated and one unregulated, the output of the unregulated one becomes a lower bound on regulated output, and the output such that "regulated" average cost equals price becomes an upper bound.[23]

In figure 16, the regulated firm perceives its marginal cost curve to be lower than that of an unregulated firm, although the true social marginal cost curve is above that of the unregulated firm because of the inefficient use of capital and labor.

THE DYNAMIC EFFICIENCY OF ECONOMIC REGULATION

Even if economic regulation creates incentives for firms to be technically inefficient, it might conceivably induce them to be more innovative than unregulated firms. Regulation usually provides some profits, if not maximal ones, that might be used for innovation. A higher rate of innovation could either lower costs over time or provide new products and services.

Suppose we include factor-augmenting terms, A and B, in the production function, optimize as before, and then do comparative statics with respect to A and B.[24] Then the optimal constrained K increases with increases in A and B. How-

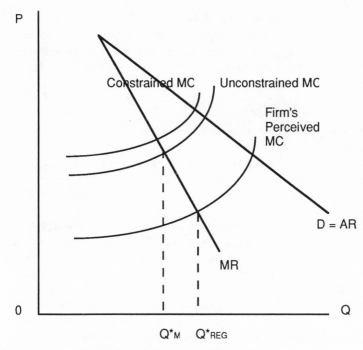

FIGURE 16   *Effects of Regulation on Equilibrium Output*

ever, factor-augmenting technological advance does not necessarily result in increased output.

Through its own R&D a firm can gain knowledge of its
innovation frontier. A profit-maximizing firm subject to
both a rate-of-return constraint and its own innovation possibilities constraint can choose more labor-augmenting technologies than it would have without regulation. Thus technological change may reinforce the bias the firm has toward
relatively capital-intensive technologies.

Innovation possibility frontiers can themselves be shifted
depending on the choices a firm makes about the scale and
direction of its R&D. If it maximizes its instantaneous rate of
constrained profit, and if the production function is homothetic, then optimal level of capital and quantity both rise.[25]
However, the R&D expenditures of the regulated firm com-

pared to the unregulated ones are ambiguous. Rate-of-return regulation can induce a regulated firm to undertake more R&D than would an unregulated one facing the same conditions. However, we cannot exclude the reverse possibility.

INNOVATION AND UNCERTAINTY

One of the major complaints about regulation is the uncertainty it creates for the firm. Coping with regulatory uncertainty decreases overall performance, increases costs, and in particular may deter innovation. For example, in the case of time-phased standards or targets, firms may be uncertain whether to choose technologies that meet current standards or to develop new ones they believe will be able to meet some stricter standard in the future. If the firm elects to meet a potentially more stringent, long-run standard, it may encounter difficulty meeting short-run standards, for its new technology will not be operational in the short run. Alternatively, new technology may not be needed if later standards turn out to be less stringent than expected, but the firm will have incurred the cost. Hedging and insurance against guessing wrongly about the reaction of the regulator runs up the firm's costs.

A regulatory agency, however, may wish to announce standards sequentially, as a function of available technologies. Since technologies may improve, this would allow more stringent future standards. Keeping its own options open preserves the regulator's flexibility. However, it reduces the firm's flexibility, since the uncertainty may increase the available options.

There is a trade-off between maintaining consistency and certainty and corrigibility. For example, in the case of sequential standards, the regulatory agency may want to set the $n+1$th standard based on actual outcomes with the nth one. However, this desire will conflict with the desires of firms for certainty. From the perspective of the firm, it is easier to treat regulation as part of a relatively fixed state of nature than it is to treat it as an interactive process or a game against the regulator.

The Foundations of Social Regulation

Environmental, health, and safety (EHS) regulation, if it is to be properly justified from an economic perspective, should derive from market failure and imperfections, just as other forms of regulation do. For EHS regulation, the failures and imperfections reside in externalities, lack of property rights, common property resources, lack of information, or asymmetries in it. For example, neither workers nor management knew until recently of the health hazards from exposure to a number of major industrial chemicals. Consequently such hazards never entered the risk calculations of labor and management. Being unknown, they could not affect bargaining in relevant labor markets. Hence wage rates did not properly reflect the actual risks from taking different jobs. Since participants did not have relevant information, unaided markets did not set the optimal distribution of workers in different occupations, nor could the wage structure be optimal allowing for different risks.

Similarly, lack of property rights or the existence of common property resources can lead to severe, perhaps irreversible damage to the environment. While the formation of markets to account for these problems might be the best public policy response, such solutions will not be technically feasible in many cases. Furthermore, some believe that setting up such markets is ethically improper, since it involves having a "bad" to trade. Trading pollution rights may provide signals that are socially undesirable—signals that pollution is just another commodity.[26] If decision makers believe such signals are socially and publicly damaging, then direct regulation may be the next best alternative.

The Economist's Perspective on EHS Regulation

Economists have three major criticisms of direct EHS regulation. First, they claim its effectiveness with respect to its primary purpose has not been sufficiently demonstrated. Here the economist's view of social regulation may have a negative bias. The benefits of EHS are hard to capture in economic accounts, especially productivity accounts; it is relatively easier to measure the direct costs of compliance and assume that indirect benefits are less than measured costs of compliance.

Second, economists claim that EHS regulation, even if effective, has significant negative externalities in that it apparently reduces productivity and diminishes the resources and incentives for product or process innovation. This claim relates to the first. Even if EHS regulation were effective with respect to its main objectives, it has negative impacts on productivity and innovation.[27] Any positive impacts on productivity and innovation do not show up in the short run. However, regulation imposes short-run costs. As a result, it is easy to argue that regulation reduces overall welfare.

EHS regulation is said to produce defensive R&D oriented to meeting standards rather than offensive R&D to find new products and processes. Furthermore, compliance uses up resources that could have been used to commercialize newly discovered products and processes. This concern about the relative increase in defensive R&D begs the question of why increased social demand for less pollution or improved health and safety do not generate offensive R&D somewhere in the economy. For example, an auto manufacturer's research on auto emissions may be considered defensive, but research to control emissions by suppliers of the manufacturer would have to be considered offensive. Offensive R&D caused by the imposition of EHS regulation should produce both new technology for compliance and new processes that satisfy EHS requirements and also increase productivity.

Third, economists claim that if the nation wants to pursue EHS regulation, it is doing so in an inefficient way. With some recent exceptions, regulators in the United States have elected to use fixed targets or absolute standards rather than price and incentive modes. At a minimum, setting standards that all firms in an industry have to meet is an inefficient (high-cost) way to achieve EHS targets compared to taxes or fees.

This uniform standards approach, economists argue, is

inequitable as well as inefficient. It applies to all firms irrespective of their capability to meet standards. Some firms have a comparative advantage over others in cleaning up their own pollution. Overall, it would be socially less costly to let the burden of cleaning up the environment fall most heavily on producers who can clean up cheaply. This can be accomplished by a system of fees or taxes to which the producers adjust according to their circumstances.

Figure 17 shows the effect of a tax on cleaning up the environment. The MSC curve shows the rising social losses from increasing pollution levels; the MSB curve shows the declining benefits to private firms (and society) of increasing pollution. If pollution costs are not incorporated in the firm's private cost calculations, they will proceed to the point where marginal benefit, MSB = 0 and marginal costs are greater than marginal benefits.

Figure 17 shows that the optimal level is not 100 percent. If society is not currently at the optimal point, the efficient thing to do is move the economy to it. Suppose the government has sufficient information to impose a tax at just the level where MSB = MSC. Then firms will equate their MB to

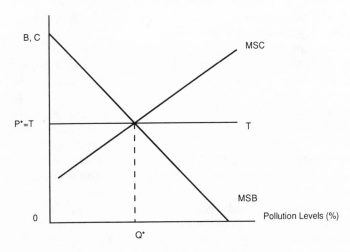

FIGURE 17   *Optimal Pollution Levels*

the tax, and the optimal pollution level P^* will result. This tax has the desirable attribute that all prices have: options can be pursued according to private interests. Enforcement costs are presumably low, and firms can adjust to their particular circumstances. In the absence of good information, however, the tax will not induce the optimal amount of pollution. It could be set too high or too low.

Legislators and administrators in the United States have consistently resisted market solutions such as fees or taxes in designing EHS regulation. There may not be sufficient information to set appropriate taxes or fees, although lack of information can well affect absolute standards too. Decision makers may have concluded that efficiency has to be overridden to achieve any kind of regulation at all. Political and administrative notions of equity hold that everyone subjected to legislation needs to be treated alike. Equity from an economic perspective requires that differential situations be treated differently.

The Dynamic Efficiency of Social Regulation

EHS regulation mainly through the imposition of standards provides incentives for innovation in technologies designed to meet EHS standards. However, it provides little or no incentive for innovation in technologies that will perform above the standard. Technology that meets a given standard, of course, may improve productivity, and being of a newer vintage, it may incorporate technological attributes not available earlier.

The more important question is the impact of EHS on general innovation. The evidence here is diverse but limited. Obviously, compliance costs divert resources from all other investments, including R&D. However, estimated returns on R&D are so high compared to other investments a firm might make that, even when a firm faces compliance costs, it need not necessarily reduce its R&D and innovation budgets.

In his macroeconomic studies Denison argues that social regulation did retard growth in income and productivity. However, the effect has not been very great, and it has decreased over time.[28] A series of studies on the pharmaceutical industry suggests that since regulation was tightened in the 1960s the rate of innovation in the industry in the United States has declined.[29] However, the regulator's response has been that the number of *effective* new drugs coming to market has not declined.

An Appraisal of Regulation

Ambiguity over Efficiency

Economic regulation in the United States was originally designed to address the pricing behavior of monopolies. Prices were too high for some stakeholders, too low and therefore predatory for others, and unstable for yet others. Furthermore, left alone, unregulated natural monopolies would not offer prices and quantities that would take advantage of scale economies. Traditional rate-of-return regulation was supposed to increase output and decrease price. Allocative efficiency probably does increase at the expense of some technical inefficiency. However, rate-of-return regulation was never designed to let regulators trade off increased allocative efficiency for decreased technical efficiency.

There seems to be no particular difficulty in finding alternative regulatory designs that would provide more incentives for efficiency than the current one.[30] However, rate-of-return regulation is so entrenched in our administrative and legal systems that change requires an unlikely consensus among all stakeholders. It is true that in the late 1970s and 1980s a consensus emerged for deregulating some industries. However, consensus about replacing the most traditional rules would be harder to obtain. Furthermore, the efficiency-inducing property of new rules would depend on the ability of regulators to monitor and enforce them. Enforcement capability varies across time from administration to administration, depending on political tastes and the current salience of the regulatory mission.

On the EHS side, standards are inefficient relative to market incentives in that the desired levels of environmental quality or safety can be achieved at a lower social cost—provided there is sufficient information. However, approaches using standards may be necessary to obtain any EHS regulation at all. Standards may be the most cost-effective instrument when information costs are counted as well as production costs.[31]

Dynamic Efficiency

Most economic and social regulation does not provide consistent incentives for innovation, and regulators have not been much concerned about their impacts on innovation. For example, cost-reducing innovations under rate-of-return regulation can increase profits, but realized lowered costs can serve as an invitation to a regulatory agency to reduce rates, thereby wiping out the profits.

The protected position of the regulated firm may itself be an incentive to innovation. A regulated firm may be in a position to appropriate benefits that an unregulated firm could not. However, its protected position may reduce its incentives to innovate. In fact, regulated firms have rarely been identified as rapid innovators.

Regulation may influence the kind as well as the level of innovations that firms pursue. Rate-of-return regulation may bring about innovations that increase sales or investment rather than decrease costs, because it is based on profits as a percentage of investment.[32]

In the case of EHS regulation, approaches based on standards provide limited incentives to innovate, since there are limited rewards for surpassing a given standard. Where regulatory agencies prefer a particular technology, any search for lower or least-cost technologies is automatically discouraged. But there is no guarantee that regulatory agencies can select socially least-cost technologies.

The administrative practices and rules that regulatory agencies use can have a significant effect on innovation. In the case of economic regulation, actual examination of rates of return and prices occurs with some lag so that, if the period between examinations is relatively long, an innovating firm can enjoy higher profits. The greater the lags, the greater the incentive, although no commission has tried to use lag as a deliberate instrument of policy. In contrast, where firms are subject to EHS regulation, lags may decrease profit and may make firms respond to high-cost standards rather than being based on actual operating experience. Some firms are exposed to both economic and EHS regulation, and different bureaus have different enforcement lags, which reflect precedent, custom, and usually limited resources. The combined impacts are hard to estimate.

Invisibility

Economic regulation by definition is not an invisible process. However, making EHS regulation invisible, through markets, by making environmental damage or the health of workers additional factors to be traded at the margin, is highly objectionable to some stakeholders.

Robustness

Regulation has not proven robust over the long run. New technology or conditions of entry frequently threaten the social performance of regulatory regimes. Although agencies have tried to cope with these, markets have replaced regulation in a number of important industries.

Timeliness

Regulation is not designed to be a timely process. At least in the United States, it is a quasi-judicial process. Regulatory agencies must gather information, hold hearings about demand and costs, and obtain the views of both the stakeholders and the interested public before making rules.[33]

The use of direct regulation requires fine tuning and adjustment, which take time, and rules that appear arbitrary and capricious may be challenged in the courts. Furthermore, indirect use of incentives and markets designed by regulators will take time to work. They may themselves produce unintended consequences that then need to be regulated.

Stakeholder Equity

The compromises among stakeholders necessary to legitimate regulation implies that static or dynamic efficiency may suffer. Few important stakeholders care about efficiency. Compromise usually means that all significant stakeholders achieve some minimal degree of satisfaction irrespective of negative efficiency impacts.

Corrigibility

The U.S. regulatory framework has not been overly corrigible. Alternatives that provide more incentive for static and dynamic efficiency have been hard to implement. The lack of corrigibility over the last decade has led to many industries becoming partially or totally deregulated. Agencies have experimented with market incentives in environmental regulation, but there has been no wide usage, and safety regulators have refined both the scope of their rule making and style.

Acceptability

The number of stakeholders who claim an interest in regulation has increased over the last twenty years. The right to participate in the regulatory process has expanded, as has the right to appeal to the courts.[34] Greater openness presumably increases acceptability and legitimacy of final rules and regulations, although the revelation of conflict or its creation could reduce it. The cost of acceptability may be a lengthy, open process that delays action however cost-effective it looks with respect to a substantive problem.

Simplicity

From the perspective of the regulatory agency, simple rules with simple information requirements mean relative ease in checking compliance. At least at the federal level, regulatory agencies will not ordinarily have the resources to process complex information. They will not have independent fact-finding and analytical capabilities concerning the economic conditions of the firms they regulate. Simplicity can, of course, conflict with other desired attributes; it may make it easier to lie and cheat. From the perspective of a regulated firm, simple rules are more easily understood and impose fewer transaction costs.

As time passes, application of initially simple rules, of

course, generates complex ones. Inevitably regulators find exceptions and meritorious exemptions. Long-lived regulatory agencies usually build up an extensive set of interpretations and administrative law that guides their decisions. It is rare for these to be reviewed from a zero base perspective. Furthermore, since firms have access to the courts, disagreements about the regulator's application of rules may generate a large body of complex legal precedent.

Information and Simplicity

Information needed to regulate ordinarily comes from those being regulated. It follows that regulation should be designed so that either (1) its effectiveness is not especially sensitive to erroneous information, (2) regulatory structures and rules prevent firms from acquiring a need and capability to lie, or (3) in the more likely case, when firms have both the capability and incentives to lie, it should provide incentives for telling the truth or penalties for not telling it.

Cost

The benefits from regulatory systems that require large-scale infrastructure and highly paid staff may be less than the costs of the system. Energy regulation in the 1970s involved large cadres of regulators as well as in-depth information about energy markets. The sheer size and scope of the regulatory operation certainly contributed to perceptions of inefficiency and ineffectiveness, if not their reality.

Even if the benefits produced by a high-cost regulatory system exceed its costs, it eventually generates constraints from sponsors, especially where the costs derive from highly paid staff. At the federal level, personnel are always scarce and at risk. Personnel freezes are common. Regulatory methods that depend heavily on staff—for example, federal inspections of the safety and quality of some foodstuffs—will always be short of the number of people and other resources required. In response, agencies will adopt rules of thumb to cut their job down to size. But there is no guarantee that these rules have any relation to socially effective regulation.

Current forms of economic regulation do not give firms

(or bureaus) much incentive for revealing true information. The actual economic state of affairs is established by agency investigations, negotiations, and formal hearings. Disputes about legitimate costs absorb much of the time and staff of regulatory agencies and run up the costs of regulation and the time it takes to regulate.

Chapter 7
Planning and Budgeting Systems

A TRADITIONAL WAY to control bureaus and their activities is to impose ex ante planning and budgeting systems on them. Once such systems reveal the preferences of bureaus and signal their future behavior, then decision makers can make correct allocations. Ex post auditing and evaluation keeps bureaus on the track selected by decision makers and provides information for the next round of planning and budgeting. Systematic inspection of outputs and inputs, if aided by well-designed budget formats, forces bureaus to discover true social objectives, to choose outputs consistent with the revealed objectives, and to select least-cost inputs for producing the outputs.

This chapter briefly describes the historical development of planning and budgeting systems, their logical foundations, and practice and pitfalls. It reviews the three most recent U.S. attempts to install systematic planning and budgeting at the federal level: program planning and budgeting (PPBS); management by objectives (MBO); and zero-base budgeting (ZBB). In addition, it discusses the ideological budgeting pursued during the 1980s. Finally, it appraises the potentials of ex ante planning and budgeting as a resource allocation mechanism.

Historical Development

In the United States, serious attempts at comprehensive planning and budgeting began at the local level in the late nineteenth century. Local political reform movements saw more rational budgeting, in particular performance budgeting, as a way to fight the political machines.[1] A performance budget is one that carries information about efficiency (e.g., costs per unit of suitably defined output) and effectiveness (the ability of the budgeted items to do a specified public job. This new efficiency and effectiveness information would prevent misuse of public funds and would help create a well-informed and outraged public willing to pursue reform.

This budgetary reform movement then spread to the federal government. In 1912 the Taft Commission on Economy and Efficiency recommended that the federal government adopt systematic budget procedures organized by decision units rather than input items. World War I generated unprecedented expenditures and debt, and centralized budgetary and allocative procedures promised to rationalize debt and expenditures. Passage of the Budgetary Reform Act of 1921 and creation of the Bureau of the Budget in the Treasury Department institutionalized an integrated federal budget and central executive oversight.[2]

As federal expenditures started to rise in the 1930s it was clear that better means of planning expenditures would have to be invented. After World War II, the two Hoover commissions made a strong case for more budget rationality and more central planning and control of the federal budget. Congress and the president were fighting constantly over the traditional line-item budget. If all parties could agree on the purposes of expenditure, then conflict could be dampened. Unordered line items, at a minimum, could be grouped by broad class of activity or by purpose. This alone would be revealing to decision makers and the public, even if the overall efficiency or the effectiveness of inputs in a class could not be measured. The bureaus requesting inputs presumably had corresponding estimates of the outputs and services they expected to deliver. Inputs grouped in relation to outputs could be used to test these estimates. Improved formats meant the sponsors could ask more probing questions, forcing bureaus to reveal and justify their estimates truthfully.

Economists believed that a bureau was like a firm in that it had an identifiable production function that showed how line-item inputs were converted into products and services.

Even if the production function could not be completely identified, then argument and debate over the rate of conversion of input to output would make for a more informed and efficient resource allocation. A budgeting system that implicitly embodied production functions would focus the executive and legislative branches on efficiency.

To defense economists in the 1960s, efficiency seemed to be the most important criterion in the design of sound force structures and, by extension, any public program.[3] If the efficient combination of military outputs could be revealed by PPBS, then service budget requests could be rationalized and the secretary of defense could make appropriate trade-offs across his entire department.

On the basis of rhetoric about its success in defense, President Johnson in 1965 extended PPBS to the entire government. The then Bureau of the Budget (now Office of Management and Budget, or OMB) and departmental planning and budgeting staffs devoted substantial effort to installing it. PPBS, however, proved far more difficult to install in civilian agencies than in the Defense Department. Serious attempts to use PPBS had withered by the time the Nixon administration took office.[4]

Instead of approaching resource allocation as a purely top-down process, the Nixon administration believed that strategic and tactical objectives of federal programs would and should reveal themselves through the management process. Instead of using PPBS, it substituted management by objectives (MBO). Resource requirements would reveal themselves in the course of rational "bargaining" between superiors and subordinates. Improved bureaucratic performance and greater central control were to result from dialogue and consensus about objectives, benefits, costs, and measures of performance. If managers at different levels jointly defined their objectives, efficient inputs and budgets required could be derived. Implicitly, all parties in the bargaining process made their own estimates of costs and benefits and had their own preferred outcomes. Consequently, MBO, as resource allocation device, became a negotiating activity, not very different from bargaining about budget increments.

The Carter administration abandoned MBO and tried zero-based budgeting (ZBB). Budgets were supposed to be constructed in terms of ranked "decision packages." Each package contained all of the activities required to carry out some known strategic objective. Within the constraint of a "critical minimum" budget for each unit, decision makers would rank their packages, thus revealing their preferences. At each budget level above the critical minimum, decision makers could then see the incremental value of adding more packages and providing additional resources. At each higher organizational level, decision makers would merge the diverse packages from lower level units, construct super-packages, and rank them. The rankings were to be done in terms of substantive merit relative to objectives at each level. Ultimately, each agency budget would consist of a prioritized list of packages. Budget authorities would then come down the list and exhaust the budget assigned to the agency.

When the Reagan administration came to power, it did away with ZBB immediately. President Reagan wanted to reduce or terminate many federal programs on ideological grounds, so he did not need any particular system of budgeting and analysis to show him which programs were ineffective. For those programs not targeted on ideological grounds, budgeting practice snapped back to traditional marginalist calculations and procedures.

FOUNDATIONS OF RATIONAL BUDGETING

The conceptual foundations for any rational budgeting scheme are as follows:

1. Some formats reveal allocation decisions and priorities better than others. At a minimum, formats that focus on outputs are superior to those that concentrate on inputs. Output-oriented budgetary systems are superior to others in maintaining a clear relation between expenditures and authorized public purposes.

2. Social performance increases when correct inputs are selected. Program implementation is easier if bureaus use correct inputs.

3. Output formats are consistent with the interests of bureaus and stakeholders, so that bureaus can and will make the necessary estimates and make them correctly. The formal structure and explicitness of output-oriented formats and their associated cost-benefit procedures limit the possibilities of strategic behavior.

4. Central budget planners hold or can obtain the right information. Bureaus have little incentive to lie about their inputs and outputs.

5. Explicitness, clarity, and transparency between inputs and outputs dampen conflict rather than increase it. Stakeholders can see how and why they disagree and then, with this newly revealed information, come to reasoned consensus.

6. Formats do not themselves change bureaus' behavior in ways adverse to the interests of sponsors and the public interest.

7. Good budgeting formats will not need to be changed, once installed.

HAZARDS AND PITFALLS

There are several routine hazards and pitfalls in implementing output-oriented budgets. For example, lack of data, overemphasis on quantification, and shortages of knowledgeable staff are always problems. But with reasonable foresight these problems can be avoided or overcome. Our concern, as usual, is with those that are unavoidable or inherent even when all parties are making their best efforts at implementation.

High Initial Transactions Costs

Every planning and budgeting system involves a particular language. Bureaus do not like new languages; they have incurred significant sunk costs in learning the old one. Transactions costs are therefore high at the beginning. The energies of budget examiners are absorbed in explaining how the syntax and semantics of a new language work. Bureaus spend much time absorbing a new language and judging how to react. Transactions costs fall later as bureaus become more fluent and hire or train their own staff to speak the particular language currently in vogue.

Diminishing Informational Returns

Although it may take them a cycle or two, most bureaus can cast their budget and justifications in any language sponsors prefer. As bureaus learn the preferred language, budget examiners must exert greater and greater effort to get the same amount of information out of the budget submissions. Eventually budget examiners burn out: they refuse to bear the increasing costs of obtaining accurate information and begin to accept the claims of the agencies and bureaus they are examining. Thus the amount of credible information generated by any budget format falls, and as it does, sponsors inevitably slide toward de facto incremental budgeting. However, as the efforts of sponsors decline and strategic behavior grows, champions of new planning and budgeting systems arrive, arguing that their new schemes will be more revealing and take less effort. Incurring a new round of transactions costs at this point seems less onerous than bearing the current operating costs, and a new cycle of budgetary reform begins.

Capture and Absorption of Planning Staffs

Any budget system keeps the planning and budgeting staffs of both sponsor and bureau busy, especially if the system is new. They may be so busy that they do not have time to pursue unstructured discussions and dialogue with operating staff, clients, and stakeholders. However, it is these discussions that provide current intelligence on whether patterns of resource allocation make sense. Since a bureau knows more about its own programs than examiners spread across many programs, eventually bureaus capture their examiners.

Decline in Corrigibility

Under line-item or input budgets, changes in programs or delivery systems may be easier than under output budgets. Pure input formats are not formally associated with given output categories. Inputs but can be scaled up or down or reallocated without formal reference back to impacts on programs or original objectives. Output-oriented budgets, by definition, have to reflect changes in inputs. Their very transparency implies lengthy transactions with sponsors and stakeholders.

Unintended Consequences of Clarity

Budgetary reform by itself does not change traditional relations or expectations between stakeholders and clients. New budget formats may reveal gainers and losers more explicitly. Budget presentations necessitate certain elaborate crosswalks and mappings from the current format to any new one. These let sponsors and clients see more clearly what has happened to the programs they have an interest in. Stakeholders who discover they are being damaged generate pressures for redress, and those who discover they have been gaining press for more gain. Hence a tighter political relation results between bureaus and their clients, and implementing efficient alternatives revealed in the budget process becomes more difficult.

NATIONAL TESTS OF OUTPUT-ORIENTED BUDGETS: 1961–1988

Federal budgetary history between 1965 and 1972 is really a history of the Budget Bureau's attempts to implement PPBS. At best it achieved moderate success. Implementation lags were natural. The bureaucracy, with a few exceptions, did not speak PBBS language. A fully realized PPBS that really matched objectives with budgets and revealed actual levels and distribution of resources as well as their symbolic and political uses would have upset longstanding routines and accommodations. Most bureaus tacitly lived with conflicting objectives and with only a loose articulation between inputs and outputs. Tight coupling reduced flexibility in response to sponsor and client pressure. Furthermore, bureaus used self-fulfilling claims appropriate for use in subverting all rational planning and budgeting systems. They argued, first, that PPBS brought no gain in substantive output or performance; and second, that transactions costs were unacceptably high.

PPBS foundered because of political and organizational naivete on the part of the PPBS designers. Relative to big, fuzzy problems of government, PPBS rarely revealed efficient choices or even prudent choices. Even if it did so convincingly, any such choice still had to make its way in a hostile political environment. PPBS was not well adapted to revealing feasible second-or third-best choices, since the political and bureaucratic information needed to do so was not in the hands of central budget planners, but was held "locally" by operating bureaus, constituents, and stakeholders.

PPBS divorced budget and allocation decisions from management decisions and from the operating bureaucrats who had to implement top-down, systemwide allocations. President Nixon believed that this divorce was inappropriate.[5] In Nixon's MBO, the highest-level managers, however, were supposed to be agents of the White House. Thus effective MBO would give the president clear control of the executive branch. If White House agents in line departments could, in fact, use MBO to achieve managerial control, then a department's strategic objectives and corollary resource allocations would have to be ultimately negotiated at the White House. Negotiation over objectives would *reveal* bureaucratic intent and achieve allocations consistent with White House aims. Thus MBO's procedural rationality would generate substantive, policy rationality. The Nixon administration never succeeded in implementing MBO fully. Though not thoroughly controlling budget and resources, the president achieved his more important objectives by going around the bureaucracy and using his White House staff in an operational role to negotiate deals and their execution, especially in national security policy.

The short-lived Ford administration was more interested in regulatory than budgetary reform. However, President Carter wanted to attack resource allocation decisions directly. On the basis of his experience in Georgia state government, on coming to the White House he mandated ZBB for the federal government.[6] Like its predecessors, PBBS and MBO, ZBB generated intense activity and thought the first time it was tried. Many argued that an annual ZBB system would not be feasible because of the uncertainties and instabilities it created, and others argued that the transactions costs were too great. Nevertheless, most agencies submitted their rankings, shaky as they might be, to OMB.

After a while, agencies adjusted to ZBB language and format. They continued to behave much as they had before, their behavior rooted in longstanding strategies and procedures that had proved satisfactory in the past and their allegiance to traditional clients unchanged. Few decision makers at the top could live with bottom-up rankings and rationales that upset clients and traditional order. Lower-level calculations based on straight cost-effectiveness could not account for higher-level strategic considerations; indeed, lower levels could not possibly know all the higher-level strategic constraints. Top managers held back on revealing these, since it helped them control their bureaus.

Paradoxically, when a bureau's supporters and adversaries gained access to ZBB rankings made at different organizational levels and compared them, longstanding deals and accommodations became clear. Once clear, they could be disputed. Different sets of rankings gave strong ammunition to OMB examiners in their never ending war to control expenditures, and rankings inconsistent with traditional resource allocation brought pressure from stakeholders. As a result, it became necessary for top managers to revise ZBB rankings so that they reflected traditional political constraints and opportunities. ZBB thus resulted in allocations that did not differ very much from incremental budgeting, but it did incur higher transactions costs.

ZBB, like PPBS, failed. Its basic premise, that bureaus had the capability and willingness to estimate their performance objectively, was flawed. Bureaucratic behavior could not be disinterested and take account of overall social objectives. Unlike previous more specific, profit-motivated applications in the private sector, it was difficult to define objectives and untangle competing claims about the effectiveness of the various program packages.[7] It could not take account of the range of political and organizational factors that constrained top level public decision makers. These factors had to be injected at the top. Since ZBB was a bottom-up process, budget officials at the center found themselves constantly correcting and retrofitting the lower-level packages and rankings. Ultimate rankings by department and agency heads had to conform to high-level policy and preferences that could not be reflected in lower-level rankings. Yet the bottom-up logic of ZBB had to be retained in arguing with sponsors. The result was a massive paper game.

IDEOLOGICAL BUDGETING

From a technical perspective there is no reason why PPBS, MBO, or ZBB cannot work when sponsors want to decrease resources instead of increasing them or when new sponsors arrive with very strong tastes and distastes about government programs. For example, given a list of decision packages constructed with ZBB, a lower budget means that a bureau will not be able to go as far down the ranked list of packages as it did before.[8] In practice, sponsors with strong ideologies, left or right, have a priori estimates about the worth of programs and therefore need not employ formats that reveal benefits, objectives, and costs as seen by the people who operate the programs. Thus in the Reagan era there were nonmarginal changes in budgets and programs based not on grounds of cost-effectiveness or rational budgeting but rather on a doctrine of minimal federal government (except for defense) and strong negative views about the worth of social programs and entitlements.

Since the administration saw the federal agencies that ran social programs as enemies, the budget formats they used to present their requests for resources made little difference. Negotiations between sponsors and bureaus are irrelevant when the sponsor's aim is to eliminate entire bureaus and departments. For this purpose, unordered "hit" lists and black books constructed by the budget officials serve as well as structured formats, and they did.[9]

AN APPRAISAL OF
PLANNING AND BUDGETING SYSTEMS

Government has to use some budget format and some procedures for allocating its finite revenues among competing programs. The output-oriented budget formats and selection of programs using a priori benefit-cost analysis have been attractive ever since government became highly complex. On their face they seem more rational than pure input formats that assign everyone small increments or decrements of resources in the vicinity of current budget.[10] Given their apparent rationality and plausibility, perhaps the most striking fact about them is that none has become a permanent feature of U.S. government. An administration can be successful and operate without them.

Ideally, output-oriented formats and their associated benefit-cost apparatus should make government allocations more efficient. They reveal the objectives and opportunity costs implicit in traditional input formats. Once revelation has occurred, agency heads and sponsors can equate the effectiveness of different programs and inputs at budgetary margins. They can act much as entrepreneurs are supposed to do inside firms.

While the output formats might push bureaus toward static efficiency, they simply were not designed to make bureaus dynamically efficient. Suppose, for example, some managers in a ZBB exercise were asked to construct some decision packages 25 percent above current budget. Their natural tendency would be to promote their previously rejected initiatives rather than to search for new services or processes. None of the budget formats provides any incentives or rewards for innovation. Conversely, addressing a loss of 25 percent would not be likely to trigger a search for innovations to run core programs at less cost. By definition, the core programs cannot be operated below the critical minimum. Although the critical minimum is dependent on the technology available to the bureau, the implicit threat in ZBB of reducing a bureau to critical minimum or zeroing it out is not likely to induce it to look hard at its current technology.

This problem of innovation is related to one of robustness. All the formats look backward. One rearranges and reorders *existing* programs or inputs until they make "sense." Most bureaus do not carry out forward scanning for emerging problems or increasing or changing demands, so that when new social demands erupt, no budget format reveals appropriate trade-offs. We can reorder existing expenditures to show what a bureau accidentally might be spending on some newly defined problem, which is certainly a good place to start. For example, we can compute how much the federal government is now spending on day care, but these expenditures cannot reveal day care programs that have been optimized through some explicit budgetary trade-off process.

We have already observed that highly rational output formats may reduce corrigibility. In chapter 2 we saw that objective functions were ambiguous and hard to identify, that a bureau could be efficient at doing the wrong thing. Output budget categories can easily entrench the wrong activities and make the correction of error more difficult.

Budgeting of any kind is a highly visible process. The communications network among sponsors, bureaus, and clients is very dense. Every agency has specialists who track the budget process on a continual basis, and every major client group employs lobbyists who do the same thing. To get what they want, bureaus and sponsors both engage in selective leaking of budget levels and distributions. Clients respond by threatening retaliation for proposed cuts, exerting pressure for increases, or by insisting that less worthy clients take cuts. Where a bureau services many clients and has many objectives, rational cost-effective trade-offs appear as deliberate intent to damage a client. Visibly reducing a program formally identified with a particular client group adds insult to injury.

Any budgeting process will eventually achieve stakeholder equity and public acceptability. There will be no budget without it. However, the sheer visibility of output categories may inhibit bargaining. Bargaining over discrete, lumpy programs may be more difficult than bargaining about highly divisible inputs such as personnel.

In the United States, federal budgets receive daily attention. If bureaus are not busy trying to acquire resources for next year, they are busy adjusting to the changes sponsors and clients have made in this year's budget. In recent years, Congress and the president have been at loggerheads over the total size of the federal budget and over budget priorities. Bureaus frequently have had to adjust plans to constantly changing authorizations and appropriations. Deep substantive disagreement between sponsors implies that no budget scheme may be adequate.

Are output-oriented budgets worth their cost? They usually are at the beginning. There are large information returns to sponsors and clients in the first or second round of implementation. No budget scheme has yet been designed that will continue to reveal important information over time. Here is the true challenge for designers of budget formats.

Chapter 8
Benefit-Cost Analysis

WHEN BUREAUS have no market guidance or signals on resource allocation, we often require them to use processes or systems designed to serve as partial substitutes. These provide information and allow clients, constituents, and public interest groups to express their views.[1] Depending on the bureau and issue at hand, government today uses many such processes, for example, benefit-cost and benefit-risk analysis, cost-effectiveness analysis, and technology assessment. Since 1969 federal bureaus whose programs or projects will affect the environment must produce reasonably well-grounded impact statements before they implement them, and they must take public views into account in policy design and rule making.[2]

All benefit-cost processes have a common logic. This logic assumes that decision makers act in the public interest, or should do so, and that they have sufficient information to identify the public interest. So, before selecting some alternative or taking an action, a decision maker estimates all the expected social benefits, measured in a commensurable way, against all the expected social costs, measured commensurably. He or she then discounts the estimated benefits and costs to the present and compares them to outcomes from some standard alternative or base case. Sometimes benefits and costs are computed in terms of risks avoided and incurred (risk-risk analysis) or in some other metric. For our purposes here, we can lump all such processes into the one general category of benefit-cost analysis (BCA).[3] Ideally, decision makers are supposed to take the information derived from

BCAs, merge them with their political and organizational intelligence, and then arrive at informed action or policy.[4]

In this chapter we examine the general logic of BCA and point out some of the major pitfalls in applying that logic. We begin with a historical sketch of BCA's development. Then to be clear, we draw a stylized, stripped-down sketch of "classical" BCA. Here all the benefits and costs of project, program, or policy alternatives are monetized, summed, and discounted to their present value. Simple comparisons and orderings of net present benefits then reveal the preferred allocation or policy change. A number of standard issues arise concerning the computation of benefits and costs and the discount rate, and the chapter describes these.

BCA is closely related to cost-effectiveness analysis and system analysis. All are processes to guide public decisions when market information is slim or nonexistent. So their appraisal takes place together at the end of chapter 10.

DEVELOPMENT OF BCA

Prudent decision makers have always calculated benefits and costs, but formal BCA can be traced to Dupuit's work on bridges in 1844.[5] He asked whether or not public investments in bridge construction were worthwhile, and to find an answer, he formulated the notion of the area under a demand curve (aggregate consumer surplus) as an appropriate measure of benefit. He defined the difference between the incremental gain in surplus attributable to the bridge and the bridge's cost as its net social benefit.

In the United States, the first interest in BCA appeared in connection with water projects. The River and Harbor Act of 1902 instructed the Army Corps of Engineers to evaluate the commercial benefits of water projects relative to their costs. In the same year, the Federal Reclamation Act, designed to open the West to irrigation, required the Bureau of Reclamation to use economic principles in its work. The 1936 Flood Control Act further required the Corps of Engineers to weigh all the identifiable benefits of its projects against their expected cost and execute only those whose benefit exceeded cost. In response to these legislative mandates, a BCA craft grew up specifically oriented toward water projects, and in the 1940s, the so-called Green Book codified the rules of the craft.[6] The Green Book led in turn to various OMB circulars and reports that standardized practice in the 1950s. Practitioners and academics codified best practice in the late 1950s and early 1960s.[7]

World War II raised unparalleled questions about the efficiency and effectiveness of military operations. Both sides were using new, untested technologies and systems. There was much room to demonstrate that alternative deployments of resources would improve performance. Many allocation problems could be attacked with "brute force" description and "back of the envelope" calculations. However, it proved fruitful to tackle some using statistical or modeling techniques. The set of formal techniques designed to improve or optimize strategic or tactical decisions came to be known as operational research in Britain and then, in the United States, as operations research (OR). OR began with very detailed descriptions and analysis of actual wartime operations, and it made relatively simple recommendations for improving performance. For example, it suggested how the new British radar installation and the RAF could improve their effectiveness against the Luftwaffe.

After the war, OR developed in two directions. In the first, it became highly mathematical, generating a number of standard problems and solution algorithms.[8] In the second, it combined with microeconomics for the analysis of large-scale, strategic military choices—for example, the composition of strategic nuclear force structure or the design of general-purpose forces. Here one or more (arbitrary) measures of performance might be selected: in the case of strategic nuclear forces, "throw weight" might be a measure. For general-purpose forces, the maximum time an army could sustain intense conventional combat might be a measure. Given agreed measures of performance, analysts would then design alternatives to existing weapons systems or deployments that promised greater performance for current costs or minimized costs for a given current performance.

Many believed that such a priori analysis should guide the production and procurement of military hardware. If the optimal combinations of military inputs could be revealed by BCA, they could then be used in rationalizing and checking service requests for budget. Indeed, the secretary of defense, given sufficient information, could himself compute the optimal budget for his entire department.

In the 1960s, cost-effectiveness and systems analysis, along with associated PPBS, were supposed to reduce the fixation of the bureaucracy and Congress on amassing inputs and focus them on efficiency—the relationship between inputs and outputs.

In the early 1970s and 1980s BCA was institutionalized in the federal government and in many state and local governments. Today most agencies have planning, budgeting, and evaluation offices whose main purpose is conducting BCAs or evaluations to feed into BCAs. A typical BCA today may be devoted to justifying what an agency wants to do rather than providing ex ante estimates on the benefits and costs of alternative courses of action. BCAs are also used to constrain agencies from taking action. Conservative administrations have used BCAs to check new regulations or to substitute weaker regulations for stronger ones. On the supply side, BCA is the hard core of university policy science programs. A substantial fraction of those trained to be policy science practitioners enters government each year, and this cadre maintains the government demand for BCAs.

The Logical Structure of BCA

We can illustrate the logic of BCA by a commonly occurring allocation problem. Suppose that someone has to make a decision from a set of relevant alternatives.[9] To choose rationally, decision makers need to know how the alternatives compare in common environments.[10] Suppose that plausible measures of benefit, performance, or effect can be identified for each alternative, and suppose that the true social costs of the alternatives can be found.[11] The true social cost of any alternative is the next best alternative that society could have obtained had it devoted the same resources to it. Then the main BCA problem is constructing a preferred ordering of the alternatives.

Commensurable information on benefits and costs makes possible a ranking of the alternatives that suffices to sift out highly costly or highly ineffective alternatives. However, since the "resolving" power of BCA models and algorithms is relatively weak, BCA comparisons will generally not be sufficient to discriminate among some residual set of good alternatives. However, reduction of a set of good and bad alternatives to only good ones, or those that appear good a priori, is a policy gain: a decision maker may not choose one of the very best alternatives but, as far as anyone can tell, he or she will not go very far wrong in choosing one of the apparently good ones.

A SIMPLE EXAMPLE

Suppose a decision maker has a budget of $150 million and has to allocate this amount among six different discrete projects or activities. Each of the possible choices is said to be meritorious by its proponents and worthy of funding, but available resources do not suffice to fund all of them, and so a choice must be made among them. Suppose also that decision makers (or the analysts who work for them) can estimate the time stream of private and social benefits from each one of the six and from each feasible combination. Suppose analysts can convert all the estimated benefits to dollar equivalents. Suppose also that the investment and operating costs of each project in each period of its life are also known.

Since public decision makers, like private ones, are assumed to have positive time preference—benefits today are worth more than benefits tomorrow, and costs today hurt more than costs tomorrow—some suitable discount factor needs to be applied to the future benefits and costs from each alternative project or feasible set of projects. Let B_{it} be the benefits of the ith project at time t, and let C_{it} be the associated cost. Let r be the discount rate believed to be relevant. Then we have:[12]

$$NPV_i = \Sigma B_{it} / (1+r)^t - \Sigma C_{it}/(1+r)^t$$

The following table shows the net present benefits and costs (in millions of dollars).

Project	Benefits	Costs
1	70	56
2	176	160
3	60	24
4	33	32
5	80	38
6	60	75

The decision maker selects the alternatives that give the greatest total sum of net present benefits within an overall budget constraint. In the example here, he or she would choose projects 1, 3, 4, 5 and just exhaust the $150 million available.[13] Project 6 decreases aggregate net benefits, and within this budget constraint, project 2 is not feasible. In fact, a budget of $118 million would capture most of the benefits. At $118 million, net present benefits would be $92 million, and at $150 million, they would be only $93 million. Instead of $150 million, a prudent sponsor might conclude that $118 million is an appropriate budget, especially if the sponsor has to face some other claimant for funds—quite a common situation.

THE MEASUREMENT OF BENEFITS

Betraying its close alignment with classical welfare economics, BCA, wherever possible, measures the impact of projects, programs, or activities in terms of the net changes in aggregated individual welfare. Wherever public activities have an impact on private markets, the worth of the public activities is measured by changes in aggregate willingness to pay, changes in consumers' surplus. Consumers' surplus is the difference between the maximum consumers are willing to pay for a commodity or service (read off a suitably defined demand curve) or are willing to do without and the amount they actually have to pay in the market. Figure 18 illustrates the concept. In the initial position C_0 on the Y-axis is both the

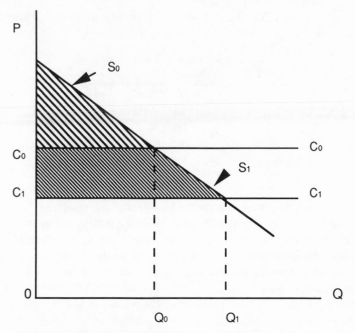

FIGURE 18   *Consumers' Surplus*

equilibrium price and marginal and average cost. From quantity 0 to Q_0, the consumer is willing to pay more than C_0. Thus the consumer surplus is S_0, the area under the demand curve above C_0 to the left of Q_0. Now suppose that a public project causes C_0 to fall to C_1. Then the new surplus is $S_0 + S_1$, the area under the demand curve above C_1, to the left of Q_1. The gain in welfare is S_1. This gain can then be compared to the cost of the project, which would be undertaken if S_1 were greater than cost. If the surpluses accrue over time, then their present value can be computed, and this can be compared to the estimated discounted costs of the project.[14]

There are four sources of difficulty in actually estimating consumers' surplus.

Specification and Sampling Errors

Estimates of willingness to pay are sensitive to the form of the demand curve. For most data sets, alternate specifications are both possible and plausible. Since the shape and locus of empirically derived demand curves will differ, there can be competing estimates of willingness to pay, and champions and opponents of a proposed public activity will seize on the estimates that favor their position. Here all one can do is proceed with econometric caution, testing the alternatives for good fit and statistical significance.[15] Best practice suggests that relevant nonstatistical information be used in specification.

Instability of Demand Curve

Demand curves can move around during a project, changing initial estimates of surplus. Some projects may be designed to create demand where none existed before, in which case one can employ sensitivity analysis to see how great any instabilities would have to be to succeed in overturning a suggested course of action. If very large instabilities would be necessary to change an expected outcome, then confidence should rise. Where small changes in shape or locus would change the outcome—say, turning a gain into a loss, one should alert the decision maker. If a proposed activity or project is reversible or can be canceled at relatively low cost, the decision maker and the bureau can prepare to react when and if new information suggests that the true willingness to pay is unfavorable to a project as it was originally conceived.

Use of the Wrong Form of Surplus

Generally consumers' surplus is computed from the ordinary demand curve. But the ordinary demand curve incorporates income effects as well as price effects, obscuring a true willingness to pay. Technically some form of compensated demand curve should be used. A compensated demand curve controls for the income effect of price changes. However, the error from using the ordinary demand curve can be bounded or a compensated curve can be computed.[16]

Suboptimization

When the prices of other goods change significantly as a result of a project, or when it affects other projects or programs that then change market prices, all of the various increments and decrements in willingness to pay need to be counted, wherever they occur. However, it is customary to limit BCA to given markets. Price effects in other markets are assumed to be small enough not to reverse conclusions based on the primary markets of concern.

Bureaus, like firms, are generally myopic. They concentrate on the effects they themselves cause directly and have a mandate to influence. If a bureau rejects projects because of negative impacts in distant markets, it will encounter criticism from its immediate clientele and constituents who stand to gain. This necessary bureaucratic myopia in estimating benefits may well lead to suboptimization or error using a willingness-to-pay criterion.

The salient question for decision makers is: would various indirect effects reverse conclusions based on the direct effects that are the responsibility of a given bureau? If so, the logic of BCA would call for a higher-order systems integration so that government as a whole acts consistently—that is, does not incur costs globally that exceed benefits. For example, if a housing project causes environmental pollution but the housing agency has no latitude or competence to deal with it, then some higher-level coordination mechanism may have to be created.[17] Of course, the effort to integrate the activities of a number of bureaus that have a stake may itself create welfare losses. Certainly, the transactions costs rise.

Pitfalls in Estimating Costs

Strictly speaking, the costs relevant to BCA are opportunity costs—that is, the benefits forgone if the same resources were allocated to the next best alternative activity. If we lived in a world where marginal cost pricing was the universal rule in both input and output markets, then the market costs of project or program inputs would give us the relevant estimate of social costs. Since we do not live in such a world, BCA usually uses direct input costs as its measure of social costs. Where these are known to be distorted, as is the case in developing countries, analysts will make some attempt at shadow pricing to correct for the distortions. In some cases, the very purpose of the projects is to change existing markets drastically or to bring new markets into being. Using existing prices as a guide to the merits of a project can lead to highly erroneous recommendations for action. What we really need are the prices, surpluses, and social costs that would result were some planned project to be successful compared to the case of no implementation. Since no one can foretell the future with sufficient accuracy to make such a comparison, economists apply different ad hoc techniques to correct for the market distortions.[18] For example, labor markets are highly imperfect in developing economies, so economists assign shadow wage rates. Similar distortions, if not so many and not so powerful, can be found in developed countries. For example, the existence of imperfect competition in most developed economies distorts market prices away from representing true social opportunity cost.

Pitfalls in Choosing Discount Rates

The benefits from a bureau's activities and many of the costs will occur over time, but decisions have to be made in the present. This year's budget ordinarily has to be expended or at least committed this year. To make a decision on allocation today, one needs the information on the future stream of benefits and costs normalized or standardized in some way. The most common way to normalize is to weight benefits and costs in the near future more heavily than those in the distant future. Benefits received today are worth more than those received tomorrow because those received today can be used immediately to earn some possible return tomorrow. Furthermore, costs tomorrow do not hurt as much as costs today, since only today's are actually incurred. Hence the time streams of benefits and costs should be deflated by some common factor, called the discount rate.

The choice of discount rate clearly affects the overall estimate of benefit-costs. The higher the rate, the less heavily future benefits and costs will be weighed. Thus a project's adversaries can claim that a high rate is appropriate, and its proponents will argue that a low one is appropriate. Welfare economics suggest using the marginal social rate of time preference derived from some present-future consumption possibility frontier and community indifference curves for present and future consumption.

Figure 19 shows a production possibility curve $Y_{t+1}\, Y_t$ for current and future output.[19] $C_{t+1}\, C_t$ is a social indifference curve. It shows the combinations of current and future consumption to which society is indifferent. Now current output can either be consumed or invested. However, output and consumption at $t+1$ depend on the level of investment at t. In figure 19, the level of current investment is given by $I_t = Y_t - C^*_t = C^*_t Y_t = C^*_t Z$, and so the productivity of capital is $C^*_{t+1}/ZC^*_t = EZ + ZC^*_t\,/\,ZC^*_t = 1 + EZ\,/\,I_t$. If we let I_t become very small, the slope of $Y_{t+1}Y_t$ is $C^*_{t+1}\,/\,I_t$, and it equals $1+r$, where r is the rate of return per unit of additional capital.

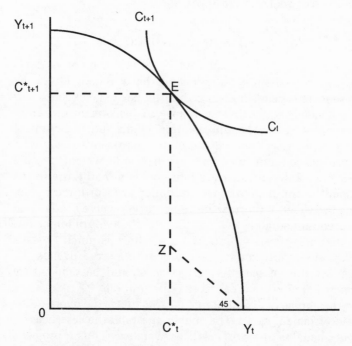

FIGURE 19   *Optimal Discount Rate*

Now the social rate of time preference s is given by the slope of C_tC_{t+1}, equal to $1+s$, since $\Delta C_{t+1}/\Delta C_t > 1$. As consumers give up C_t (society invests more), they require more and more consumption in the future C_{t+1}, to remain on C_tC_{t+1}. At the point of tangency E, $s = r$. The rate of return on investment must just equal the rate savers require.

In practice, this rate is hard to calculate. Thus decision makers use rates that can be easily obtained, for example, rates of return on private sector investments or market rates of interest. For the federal government, OMB picks a discount rate that it believes is reasonable, such as 10 percent. It then applies this rate uniformly to prospective projects in all agencies, providing a common base for comparison. The unavailability of the true discount rate puts the economy in a second-best position away from E. However, if some second-best r seems too far off from stakeholders' perceptions of the true r, we know that decision makers will hear from them through political channels.

BCA and Decision Making

Tests for the utility and credibility of BCA concern whether errors will be made in following recommendations and what the costs of the errors will be. The decision maker wants to know—or should want to know—how far off the estimates would have to be to reverse some recommended action or policy. Since this cannot be known a priori, many rules of thumb have evolved from practice to avoid bogging down. Some of the more important ones are listed below.

A Fortiori Assumptions

A decision maker can use that set of reasonable assumptions most *unfavorable* to a prospective program or project, that is, to apply assumptions that understate benefits and overstate costs. If, in this most unfavorable situation, BCA still suggests that some project or program is worthwhile, then there is greater confidence that performance will be adequate in circumstances better than the most unfavorable.

The most unfavorable circumstances seldom occur, but even if they do, the decision maker has some warrant and justification for an original decision.

A fortiori arguments, of course, are limited by what one imagines as the most unfavorable. Military history provides the starkest examples. Long before World War II, U.S. military planners envisioned conflict with Japan. However, the most unfavorable scenario did not include a surprise attack on Pearl Harbor with significant loss of most of the Pacific fleet. Failures to anticipate unfavorable cases are extremely common in the deployment of complex technologies. For example, even though NASA had the information to consider a worst case for its space shuttle—a destructive explosion on launch with loss of life—it never analyzed such a contingency and the potential consequences for the agency. It interpreted its information in such a way that the risk of the worst case was always low enough not to worry about it. A long series of successful launches reduced the subjective risks of NASA decision makers.[20] Similarly, even though major risk and fault assessments of nuclear power reactors are common in the United States, no one envisioned the sequence of human and mechanical error at Three Mile Island,[21] and the Soviet decision makers did not or would not consider the kind of case that occurred at the Chernobyl nuclear power plants in 1986.

Testing for Dominance

One project or program may dominate the alternatives, that is, in practically all imaginable environments one outperforms all others on salient criteria. Dominance is shown in figure 20. Present net benefits are shown on the Y-axis, and an index of the overall environment is shown on the X-axis. Alternative 1 dominates alternative 2. Given some apparent dominance, one can examine the assumptions and variations needed to reduce the performance of the dominant alternative to that of the second best one or below. If only extreme perturbations reduce dominance, then decision makers may reasonably conclude that they should select the dominant one.

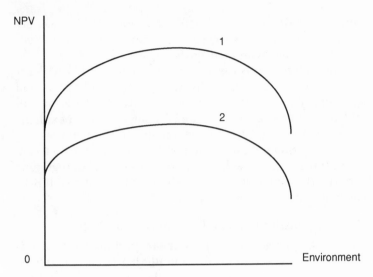

FIGURE 20   *Dominance Relation*

Testing for Equality of Outcomes

Where no reasonable variations in assumptions produce any difference in expected performance between alternatives, decision makers can be indifferent between them. Then they can select the one that meets the most criteria not included in the original BCA—for example, equity or political requirements. For example, two projects may have equal performance profiles, but one may have superior distributional properties. More of the benefits may go to individuals or groups of special concern: if, say, the poor are of special concern, then one can justify choosing the project that sends proportionally more benefits to them.

Testing for Time

Two projects may appear to have the same BCA outcome. However, they may have very different benefit and cost time streams. Prudent decision makers cannot be indifferent to these. Certainly, if most of the benefits will be realized long after decision makers have left office, and the most signifi-

cant costs will be incurred while they are still in office, bureaucratic prudence suggests that they select alternatives
with early benefits and late costs.

Alternatives with early costs and late benefits will encounter continuous difficulty with budget authorities and
sponsors. Implementing them can easily affect the overall
budgetary and strategic posture of a bureau, which explains
in part why bureaus have to be oriented to short-run results.
Few in government are charged with the care of the long run;
hence few managers will champion activities with high long
run payoff but high short-run costs, even though overall BCA
calculations may be favorable.

Testing for Institutional and Organizational Costs

BCAs do not generally count the institutional and organizational costs of implementing the alternatives revealed to be
superior. Implicitly they assume that bureaus are willing
enough and competent enough to implement the superior
alternatives. Yet it is quite possible, and frequently prudent,
to choose the second- or third-best alternative because its
implementation costs would be lower or because it is far
more feasible politically than the first choice suggested by
standard a priori computations.

ALTERNATIVE SOURCES OF INFORMATION

BCA, on the benefit side, tries to estimate true social
willingness to pay (derived ultimately from the individual
utility-maximizing model of microeconomics). But economic
estimates of willingness to pay are not the only sources of
information about public tastes. For any significant project or
program, there will be a large flow of information from political channels: clients, constituents, and interest groups will
let decision makers know directly about the perceived worth
of a program. In particular, the expected losers will make
their views known. These expressions of worth can be
checked against what BCA says.[22] For a number of problem
areas such as the environment and pollution, decision makers must obtain formal expression of citizens' judgments and

cannot proceed without them. If these judgments are consistent with BCA recommendations, then confidence in the latter's recommendations should increase. If they are not consistent, then a decision maker can make further enquiry as to why they disagree.

Chapter 9
Cost-Effectiveness and Systems Analysis

THE RANGE of applications in BCA covers projects, programs, and policies whose results show up in price and quantity changes in relevant markets. So willingness to pay can be computed. Where there are no such markets, decision makers use cost-effectiveness or systems analysis (SA).[1] These are a priori, rational procedures for raising questions about complex systems that we must operate under uncertainty or ignorance.[2] At their core they use the same basic concepts as BCA and have the same objective—maximize effectiveness for given cost or minimize cost for given effectiveness. However, measures of effectiveness or performance are not related to market outcomes, but defined by the decision maker. Performance is determined by manual or computer models, not by market changes in consumers' surplus.

Often the system of interest will be large, messy, and only partially understood. There will be ambiguity or uncertainty about the environments in which it will have to operate. In some cases, costly systems must be procured and deployed without much real-world testing. For example, the United States spends enormous sums building and maintaining its strategic nuclear capability. A true test of the investment in this capability would be (1) its ability to survive a first strike from a determined, intelligent adversary; and (2) its ability, were a first strike to occur, to provide flexible, controllable options for decision makers. But this is a test no one ever wants to bear. While other public systems may not involve such stark uncertainty, many do involve large-scale investments under conditions of uncertainty or ignorance. No market will give us additional information, and no contingent markets can be set up to handle the uncertainty. One therefore turns to SA.

Stylized Components of Systems Analysis

SAs, like BCAs, have a logic, although the actual sequence in constructing them may not correspond to it. This logic states that one should first specify the objectives and the resources available to attain the objectives. Within the given resource constraints, one next constructs or designs alternative means of carrying out the objectives. one then evaluates the alternatives using some analytical device, most frequently a well-calibrated mathematical model or simulation. Given the emergence of one or more superior alternatives, one goes on to conduct sensitivity analysis to see how well the preferred alternative stands up in off-design circumstances and whether the choice of alternative should be switched.[3] One then reexamines the initial objectives, resources, strategies, and alternatives and adjusts them. If these are inconsistent, one redoes the SA. So, in this iterative way, SA eventually matches up the objectives, budgets, and systems that should be preferred with currently held information.

In practice, the analytical process can start anywhere. A lack of feasible alternatives relative to some objective may trigger an examination of objectives. Disputes about objectives may lead to changes in budget levels and, consequently, to a search for new alternatives. Changes in technology may force changes in both alternatives and budgets. Quite frequently SA reveals that objectives are unreal or poorly specified or that the resources needed to reach strongly desired objectives are far greater than estimated.

A Stylized Example:
The Strategic Defense Initiative Background

In March 1986, President Reagan proposed R&D efforts that were to culminate, he hoped, in a highly effective and affordable ballistic missile defense (BMD). BMD had always had strong advocates in the United States, but in the past it always appeared that the offensive capabilities available to the Soviet Union would negate any BMD that was technically feasible and affordable. The president's proposal drew strong support and strong opposition.[4] From an SA perspective it is important to untangle the substantive issues, claims, and questions and to organize information about them. Since the architecture of the strategic defense initiative (SDI) is still uncertain and different architectures have strong proponents and opponents, identifying questions that can be decided now and those that can be decided later is also a part of the SA job.

The Ideal Analysis of SDI

Ideally, a complete SA would embed alternative SDI architectures and systems in the overall U.S. strategic nuclear posture, and it would embed plausible and feasible Soviet responses in alternative Soviet postures. Then the alternative pairs of overall strategic postures would be "exercised" under different scenarios to determine relative outcomes. Outcomes might be measured in actual expected losses on both sides, residual damage potential, long-run economic viability, and so forth. For example, net damage potential curves like the ones in figure 21 lie at the heart of quantitative calculations about strategic nuclear forces.

Figure 21 shows an abstract "damage potential" for the United States and the Soviet Union should a certain weight of attack actually be delivered (here measured in weapons reliably delivered). To estimate performance from the curves, one takes account of the reliabilities and target kill probabilities of all the systems in a given force structure and computes the expected number of weapons that would survive and explode.[5] Then one reads off the damage potential.

Alternative pairs of strategic nuclear forces would, of course, cost different amounts over a given time. So systems analysts have to make comparisons involving unequal effectiveness and unequal cost. There is no simple way to make such comparisons. The analysis of outcomes is sometimes

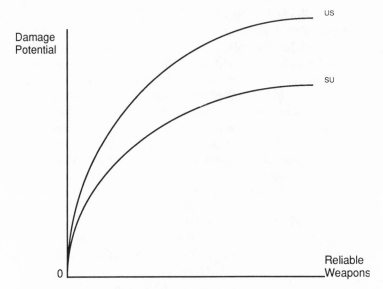

FIGURE 21   *Damage Potential Curves*

standardized by using an equal cost constraint. For example, the introduction of SDI into U.S. strategic forces and the Soviet response could be constrained to expected strategic nuclear expenditures over five or ten years, on the assumption that no strong interaction would change expenditures over those years.

The ideal SA would go on to discuss the likely side consequences of these fully embedded postures, including political consequences with respect to allies, clients, and adversaries. Ultimately, the analysis would come down to some overall, summative recommendation of developing and deploying SDI.

The Actual SDI Debate

So far the SDI debate has not approached the ideal: the strategic consequences have taken a back seat to arguments over the technological feasibility of the components and the overall feasibility of a system.[6] Thus opponents argue that it will never be technologically feasible to deploy a reliable, effective BMD, and, even if it were, in the circumstances *most favorable* to it, its deterrent value and its damage-limiting potential would be negligible. It still would always be feasible and cheap for an adversary to negate any BMD the United States deploys. Proponents, in contrast, argue that in circumstances *most unfavorable* to BMD, the additional uncertainty and cost imposed on adversaries would both enhance deterrence and reduce ability to inflict damage on the United States. Such an outcome would enhance U.S. threat potential in international crises.

It is hard to estimate the merits of these competing a fortiori arguments. Only partial strategic outcomes have been estimated where the performance of an SDI was matched against the actual Soviet strategic nuclear posture or some plausibly enhanced one. In any case, much of the actual debate turns not on the predicted performance of BMD in saving lives, production potential, or U.S. strategic weapons but on arguments over the arms race dynamics. SDI, because of its characteristics as they would be perceived by the Soviets, opponents argue, would be self-defeating and self-negating. Either the Soviets would take countermeasures with respect to their ICBMs, or they would preserve their strategic nuclear capability in some other way, for example, by increasing their submarine-launched cruise missiles. In either event, the United States would respond, generating a new upward spiral in the arms race. Thus no one will be any safer, and resources that could have been used for increasing economic performance or social welfare will have been used up. Furthermore, SDI makes strategic systems much more complex. As the number and complexity of weapon systems increase, the ways nuclear war can arise increase and some accident is highly likely to occur.

Proponents of SDI argue that it magnifies adversaries' planning and design problems and, thereby, their social opportunity costs. In particular, the United States can outrace the Soviets so that, even if they respond to a U.S. deployment and try to negate SDI, the United States can preserve deterrence and threat potential.

No one, however, knows about the dynamics. Strategic arms races do not always occur when one adversary increases deterrent capability nor are strategic arms races necessarily evil: very small, homogeneous strategic forces on both sides may be far more vulnerable than large diversified ones, and a race to increase and diversify strategic forces may therefore be stabilizing. Since the dynamics are unpredictable, at a minimum R&D and sufficient testing should continue to keep options open, rather than automatically foreclosing them. Deployment of SDI might then be used as a bargaining chip in arms control negotiations.

THE ROLE OF SA IN THE SDI DEBATE

No true systems analysis has yet appeared in the open literature.[7] But the quantification of outcomes with different BMD systems embedded in the overall structure of strategic nuclear forces would focus current debate about nuclear strategy, and budgets. Arguing about expected outcomes may be superior to arguing about inputs, and there may well be surprises. For example, SDI's deployment may not make any difference at all, given opposing force structures fully adapted to it.

Showing with some precision how and why there is disagreement on policy or procurement is one important function of SA. Another is showing the limits of a priori reasoning about future systems. There may be no adequate analytic to describe the dynamics of strategic nuclear arms races. Here one can untangle competing beliefs and test them for their logic and consistency. Furthermore, in the face of uncertainty that cannot be resolved, SA may reveal postures and processes that could be employed as hedges. The preservation of options for later decision may itself become an important criterion, and SA can point out the value of doing this.

Pitfalls in Practicing SA

Good systems analysis is defined by the consideration and avoidance of generic pitfalls. It is easier to describe these then to give universal rules for carrying out SAs, and so we turn to some of the more common ones.

Suboptimization

The objectives that decision makers initially believe important may be too narrow in scope. Certainly the design of the federal bureaucracy encourages a concern with one's own bureau. The higher-order objectives that most bureaus say they exist to serve will be displaced by achieving the things that they know how to do and for which they have operating responsibility. As a result, the specification of objectives frequently and naturally follows current organizational structure, even though the proper objective, in a substantive sense, cuts across organizations. Thus the navy pursues the objective of increasing the size and capability of its carrier task forces, and the air force pursues the objective of increasing its land-based tactical air strength. But both of these objectives can be subsumed under the more global ones: to deter conventional warfare and crisis and, if deterrence fails, to be able to carry out conventional operations that lead to satisfactory political results. One can probably fight a conventional war by giving the navy the large carrier forces it prefers and the air force the large amount of tactical air it prefers. But the same capability could be achieved at less cost if trade-offs were organizationally possible.

Similarly, housing and health programs and services can be related to the overall objective of reducing poverty. But these are generally administered by different agencies. Interagency planning and coordination efforts are one response to trade-offs at the federal level, but they work only fitfully. Serious coordination means giving up some organizational prerogatives.

Inappropriate Choice of Models

Systems analysis needs models that relate objectives, resources, and alternatives to expected real-world outcomes.

There are two ways to design these: one can construct either broad, general-purpose, relatively complex models that address many different questions, or one can build detailed models to answer sharply defined questions. There are trade-offs between the two types. Truly general-purpose models have greater scope but less resolution than question-specific ones. Question-specific models give sharper resolution on the questions they were designed to answer, but for every new set of questions, one may have to construct a different model.

There is also a trade-off in the confidence one can have in the results. Large-scale models with lots of internal feedback take many more factors into account. However, causal chains are much more difficult to track, and it is hard to determine whether a reported result comes about because of real-world factors or the quirks of model builders. Question-specific models highlight fewer variables, but causal chains are easier to track. There are usually no truth or falsification tests for either kind. The ability to keep track of causal chains and to explain and justify outcomes in relation to assumptions and parameters becomes an important partial substitute for tests of verification.

Lack of Attention to Organizational History and Culture

Systems analysis says that if organizations behave in the optimal prescribed way, there will be an improved outcome relative to some problem they have. But in deriving optimal behavior for bureaus, SA abstracts from their organizational and political history. There is then no test within SA of ability to implement the technical solutions it suggests. Bureaus generally resist change and innovation even if they know it will be cost-effective, so the set of feasible, optimal, and implementable solutions may be very small. Current organizations were never designed to carry out solutions derived from SA, and they will have few internal champions. More effective alternatives are not necessarily acceptable to implementing bureaus, and they may be seen as threatening, in which case they will not be implemented at all. Mildly threatening ones will only be implemented slowly. Yet SA provides little guidance on the incentives required to make bureaus implement cost-effective alternatives.

Utilization

Systems analysis is moderately or marginally reformist. Its aim is to make those with power more rational, although its actual payoff may only be in making stakeholders aware of issues and potential solutions. Given such an intention, there must be some translation between the technical analysis and recommendations, since the language of decision makers is not the language of analysis. The former is not subtle. It boils down the contribution of any kind of analysis to the substance of an issue, the recommended actions, and the possible organizational and individual gains. In contrast, the language of SA must obviously be complex, qualified, and contingent. Messages for decision makers have to be compressed and simple but still give some sense of the qualifications and contingencies.

A PRIORI APPROACHES VERSUS LEARNING BY DOING

BCA and SA modes for improving decision making can be contrasted with more process-oriented approaches, which provide guidance on organizational design and processes. If a bureau designs the right decision processes, it will make reasonable decisions. Whatever problems and alternatives it faces, procedures and processes should *reveal* the correct things to do, since no a priori BCA or SA can cover the range of problems bureaus will actually encounter. A good decision is one arrived at by organizational processes and procedures that provides satisfactory, if not perfect, outcomes for most internal and external stakeholders. In a world where objectives are hard to define or are left deliberately vague and murky, a good decision process reveals and defines objectives as well as the means of implementing them.

The a priori approach of BCA and SA can, of course, be an integral part of any process for making decisions. For example, the federal government now tries to compute the expected economic benefits and costs of proposed environmental and safety regulations. Such computations cannot guarantee the selections of alternatives that will be socially optimal, but they serve to focus bureaus, sponsors, and stakeholders on substantive issues. And they create some new stakeholders—the analysts—whose special interests lie in achieving cost-effectiveness and efficient allocation of resources.

An Appraisal of BCA and SA

BCA and SA are processes to give decision makers sufficient information so that they can make efficient and effective allocations if they want to. BCA and SA offices exist in bureaus to increase the desire to do so. They do not themselves allocate resources or deliver goods and services like markets or bureaus.[8] So here I appraise them in terms of their ability to induce decision makers to meet the ten criteria laid out in chapter 2.

BCAs are designed to reveal efficient alternatives, that is, those with net present social benefits greater than zero. If we can compute social benefits and costs reasonably accurately, then allocations derived from BCAs should be more efficient than those derived in other ways. Even without accurate computations, the search for social benefits and costs, if carefully checked and validated, forces decision makers to think seriously about efficiency. There are, of course, cases where agencies invoke BCAs and SAs to justify preferences based on other grounds. And it is not unknown for BCA experts to tell decision makers what they want to hear. But sound craft rules and ethical codes should curb such tendencies.

Traditional BCAs undervalue the future in the public sector just as return-on-investment (ROI) calculations undervalue it in the private sector. Allocations and policies with high future benefits but which require high current costs will not ordinarily rank high in any BCA calculus. If having adequate future options is a social benefit, then using BCAs and SAs as our sole or principal decision-making tools is not prudent.

Sensitivity analysis in BCA and SA is supposed to flag decision makers on the robustness of the alternatives they confront. But sensitivity analysis is only as good as the models and computational algorithms we can construct. Since we use BCA and SA in situations where we have little direct experience and lack complete understanding, a priori assertions about robustness of alternatives need to be guarded. Analysts need to make clear the critical assumptions they used in evaluating alternatives.

Timely allocations and policies require timely information. BCAs and SAs need to arrive when decisions are made. However, neither decision makers nor analysts can ever completely specify a priori the kinds of information that will be salient. The terms in which decisions will be made rarely stay constant. As insurance against having no information, analysts may embark on general programs of work and research which they believe relevant. But actual relevance requires hard work and good communication between analysts and decision makers.

Any actual choice of programs, technologies, or regulations involves bargaining and negotiations with stakeholders. Bargaining and negotiation generally exhibit little concern for overall social impacts (although a complete lack of concern may mobilize a bureau's adversaries). The existence of a priori, rational processes that bureaucracies must use and the organizational presence of agents with a vested interest in such processes serve as a partial counter to the routine adjustments, accommodations, and allocations made in achieving stakeholder equity. Stakeholders with vested interests in BCA now have to be given equity along with others.

BCA and SA also introduce a degree of competition into the decision-making process, since competing organizations and bureaus feel compelled to offer up their own analysis. Thus BCA and SA become ways to obtain more information and reveal critical assumptions and political and bureaucratic sensitivities. They can also be useful political tools in balancing the demands and threats of special-interest groups.

BCAs and SAs do not generally weight alternatives according to their corrigibility or simplicity. These are considered more the properties of organizations that will implement the BCAs, not values to consider in computing benefits. BCAs are just as likely to rank noncorrigible and complex alternatives higher than corrigible or simple ones. They are not inherently self-reflective about the errors that may occur if decision makers take them seriously and act on them. One may argue that when significant social error occurs, new BCAs can be undertaken to guide action. However, since sunk costs matter a lot to public bureaus, they can easily be locked in. It is unlikely that erroneous allocations or policies are going to be overturned because of newly revised BCAs and SAs.

Allocations and policies based on BCAs and SAs often have difficulty gaining public acceptability. Some interested party can always claim that a BCA underestimated benefits or overestimated costs. When allocations impinge on values, invoking BCAs and SAs to make complex social decisions generates intense controversy and opposition.[9] BCAs that impinge on human life and the environment have particular difficulty in gaining acceptance.

Chapter 10
Demonstration, Experiment, and Evaluation

SOME PROSPECTIVE POLICIES or programs represent major departures from current practice. So a priori modes of analysis and program selection cannot be sufficient to clarify choice. They provide information about small perturbations around the status quo and necessarily have less to say about new programs not yet tried or old programs in radically new environments. Economic theory, for example, suggests that a negative income tax would cause reductions in hours of work offered. A critical question in implementing such a tax would be whether reductions would be large or small relative to what might be economically and politically bearable, but there may be no social experience or evidence relevant to the effects of such a tax on hours of work.

To get information about the effects, we could survey potential recipients on how they would behave if they were given additional resources. However, it is unlikely that such surveys would be definitive, for people act differently in real-life situations from the way they predict they will act in answering a survey questionnaire. We could try to construct econometric models of work behavior and estimate or simulate the effects of the tax. However, the data for estimating the model would come from a world that had never had such a tax. The estimates from the model would not be credible, and the model's specification and parameters would be subject to challenge. In contrast, randomized social experiments that tracked people who received alternative payments and recorded their actual work behavior would allow rigorous inferences about causality and impacts.[1] Instead of selecting policies or programs with little immediate information, decision makers can embrace a "try it and see" approach, ranging from uncontrolled demonstrations, to "proof of concept," to highly controlled, randomized experiments. If it is technically and politically feasible to wait for more information, and if the transactions and operating costs of experiments or demonstrations are low, decision makers can test new technologies or programs in the field. In principle, they can use new, high-quality information about effectiveness to determine the design of their programs and the deployment of resources.[2]

This chapter discusses demonstrations, experiments, and evaluations as strategies for decision making. It provides a brief history, describes logical foundations, and lists the pitfalls. Our notion of pitfalls is the same as that outlined in earlier chapters. We have to worry about the pitfalls and difficulties that remain even when experimental and evaluation designs meet standards of best practice.[3] Then the chapter presents an overall appraisal using the criteria listed in chapter 2. The term *evaluation* among social scientists has been restricted to finding the impacts of ongoing or proposed social programs, but this is too restricted a usage for the purposes here. For example, procurement of weapons systems always involves a final *evaluation* phase. Evaluation concepts and tools extend far beyond social programs.

Origins of Evaluation Strategies

Field testing and experiment for industrial products and technologies have long been common and necessary. Major new products have to be tested in sample markets because initial demand estimates are highly uncertain. New industrial processes have to be tested because there are always technological and economic uncertainties related to increased scale or scope. Physical behavior is not always linear, and there may be unexpected interactions between technologies and the people who will operate them.

In the defense sector, the testing and evaluation of military hardware in simulated battle conditions is a desirable norm. Many believe that field test and demonstration of competitively developed prototypes is the best way to determine cost-effectiveness. New technologies frequently seem excessively risky to the private sector, and so the federal government undertakes demonstration and development work to reduce the uncertainties—for example, in agriculture, aircraft development, and nuclear power. When commercialization of an invention would lead to social benefits that are deemed greater than private benefits, the federal government builds pilot plants and provides information to reduce risks and costs.

The modern program evaluation movement argues that suitably designed social experiments and evaluations can be as "hard" as technological ones. Toward the end of the nineteenth century, social scientists began claiming that analysis of economic and social data could help in choosing between alternative public policies and programs. Most data came from "natural" experiments in executing budgets and programs. Routine transactions were recorded in primitive accounting formats, never designed for analyzing costs or effectiveness. However, social scientists believed that suitable translation and aggregation would reveal whether outcomes could be attributed to policies or programs.

Efforts by social scientists to enter the policy arena gained momentum during the Roosevelt and Wilson eras. Innovations in social and economic programs naturally increase demand for evaluation.[4] In the 1930s, the New Deal undertook many ad hoc social interventions and demonstrations, and questions about their efficiency and effectiveness were naturally raised. At the same time, statisticians and social scientists perfected the theory and practice of large-scale sample surveys and refined multivariate statistical procedures. Thus it became technically feasible to obtain reliable firsthand information about program impacts on the intended beneficiaries. Given true randomization or well-designed statistical controls, sampling permitted valid inferences about how entire populations would respond to programs. During World War II and after, social science and economics continued to develop sophisticated tools and models, until, by the 1960s, social scientists believed their research technologies were powerful enough to cast light on major policy interventions.

This same period saw a sharp rise in demand for information on the effects of policy interventions. The federal government found itself attacking the nation's most difficult social problems simultaneously.[5] Since the federal government was trying many new things, experiment and evaluation seemed substantively rational and they could also be used as important political selling points. So government's demand for all kinds of program evaluation increased greatly, but especially for poverty and education programs.[6] In many cases, social scientists had a hand in designing the new programs. To them it was only natural to inject an evaluation component into each. Winning a war on poverty or illiteracy required some degree of efficiency and effectiveness; otherwise resources would be wasted. Maintaining political support also required some degree of efficiency. Support and resources had to come from the middle and upper classes, and they eventually would demand value for money.

Few doubted that social scientists could produce the evidence required if they used modern tools—social and psychological tests and surveys, randomized social experiments, or near substitutes. Indeed, some optimists argued that society would be far better off if it always based policies and programs on information from well-designed evaluations and experiments. More could be learned in this rigorous way than by trying to discover the always ambiguous lessons of policy failures.[7]

By the 1970s, however, society was no longer interested in warring on social problems. Washington's major policy problem was changing producer and consumer incentives to conserve fossil fuels and encourage pollution abatement. Energy and pollution problems did not lend themselves to large-scale social experiments or demonstrations, although there were a few aimed at reducing the demand for energy. In any case, it had become clear that social science and economics simply did not have sufficient resolving power to provide definitive results, even under optimal experimental conditions.[8]

In the political retrenchments of the 1980s, demand for new programs was low. The Reagan administration strongly believed that an excess of government programs was the nation's most important social problem. It believed that social scientists were really disguised social engineers, and so it cut funds for all social programs. Any desire for rational social policies derived from well-planned demonstrations and experiments could certainly be made consistent with a conservative administration and free-market approaches to social problems. However, the administration was not attracted to any notions of an experimenting society, although it continued to fund some demonstrations and experiments.[9] These were smaller in scale, and their purpose was improving the residual social programs that the administration felt were worthwhile and appropriate.

LOGICAL FOUNDATIONS

Suppose that decision makers are considering a new program with a few *real* objectives.[10] Suppose that the program has few antecedents and that demonstrations or experiments seem to be an appropriate option. The logic of experiment and evaluation is as follows.

Two Chief Assumptions About the Policy Environment

1. Decision makers can afford to wait for information from evaluation. In other words, the political and social costs of waiting for improved information are less than the costs of not waiting, of acting on partial information and then adjusting.

2. The policy environment remains sufficiently stable for the evaluations and experiments chartered at a particular time to remain technically feasible and relevant to policy over time. In cases where there are shifts in the environment, some of the original questions remain relevant, and demonstrations or experiments still have sufficient momentum to

continue. Thus the connection between policy questions that decision makers want answered and demonstrations or experiments is clear and remains stable.

Technical Assumptions

3. Randomized experiments are always the best option to obtain information for decision making. They provide the most reliable information about impacts of a program. Essentially, this means that program targets or recipients are randomly assigned to treatment groups. If the first-best experiment is not feasible or is inappropriate, there exists a second-best one that will deliver a reasonable amount of consistent information if the design is implemented as planned.[11]

Implementation Assumption

4. Whatever evaluation design is chosen, its actual implementation in the field will not differ too much from the one planned.

If this assumption is not met, the ability to make statements about the population's response to alternative treatments will be compromised. However, it is frequently difficult to apply treatments as designed. At some point clients and constituents may force change or adjustments to get experimental treatments fully implemented. A sponsoring agency can have strong incentives for violating an original design. When apparently valuable lessons and program guidelines show up early, an agency may be tempted to begin changing its programs either on grounds of cost-effectiveness or for bureaucratic gains.[12] Obviously, if agencies adjust their programs on the basis of partial information and short-run lessons, they will compromise the substantive purpose and technical design of an experiment or evaluation.[13] Furthermore, short-run lessons may not be the true lessons: some initially positive outcomes may turn out to be negative over the long run and vice versa. However, given the short-run perspective of most bureaus, there may be little inclination to wait until definitive results show up.

FAILURES AND PITFALLS

Weak Policy Credibility

No matter how well designed, experiments, demonstrations, and program evaluation will not be definitive.[14] Proponents of programs with bad experimental outcomes or evaluations always argue that the experiments or evaluations were faulty: for them the evaluation does not capture important positive spillovers or improvements in program process, or they argue that positive effects will be observed in the long run if only the program were allowed to continue a while longer. Opponents of programs with positive evaluations argue the reverse: for them, small detectable negative effects only get worse over the long run, and evaluators constantly overestimate positive spillovers.

Moral Hazards

Results of evaluation provide incentives to agencies to avoid serious evaluation. There are few rewards for willingness to undertake them: managers are not selected on this basis and those who do undertake them will be criticized as acting against their bureau's interests. Sponsors may reduce budgets, and adversaries will claim they can deliver the same services better. Positive evaluations suggest a bias in favor of a bureau, and such claims are difficult and costly to disprove.

Sponsors observing managers' reluctance to evaluate programs then turn around and penalize the agency, with the result that it becomes embroiled in political and technical controversy. Paradoxically, evaluation processes designed to make rational choice more likely end up reducing its likelihood.

Timeliness

An original set of decision makers may agree that the best social policy depends on the results of experimentation or evaluation and may well be willing to delay action until results arrive. However, the tenure of decision makers is usually short relative to the time required for technically valid results. As decision makers are replaced, natural shifts of attention and interest occur, and the articulation between demonstrations and experiments and policy becomes weaker. Support for ongoing experiments will erode no matter how strong it was originally. Finding themselves with now irrelevant evaluations and experiments, a new set of decision makers will attempt to change the designs or questions, trying to extract information relevant to them from ongoing work never designed for this purpose. New decision makers usually mean a change in overall policy environment. So experiments or additional treatments never dreamed of originally may be especially salient. But injecting them compromises the validity of previously designed experiments.

Costs

Social experiments and evaluations cost more than any other means of acquiring information, but at best they can answer only a few questions. The more questions posed, the more complex the design, the higher the costs, and the more visible to sponsors they become. As their costs and visibility rise, the perceived benefits of the alternative programs and information forgone for their sake rise also. As time passes decision makers and evaluators will be tempted to reduce the scale and scope of experiments and evaluations on grounds of cost. But reductions in scale and scope will cause significant information to be lost; for example, evaluators may reduce the number of control groups, reducing the power of an experiment to be generalized.[15]

APPRAISAL

From a social perspective, program evaluations and experiments should be considered as processes for designing more effective and efficient programs over the long run. They should be viewed as devices for changing the terms of public debate and as a means of changing agency culture.[16] Most policy questions and issues come around again, and the specific results and all the background information can then be used. In fact, the results may trigger a search for innovative new policies or programs.

Short-run program or policy emergencies usually generate demands for experiments or demonstrations. But most emergencies will be over long before experiments or demonstrations have been completed; and those who decided to embark on them will have left office long before the information arrives. Some other emergency will be important to current decision makers. Thus evaluation information cannot be timely.

Even large-scale experiments and evaluations can answer only a few questions over a long time, even when or because they are properly designed and implemented. However, their corrigibility and controllability are perhaps overly high. It is relatively easy to shut off their flow of funds. Any budgetary stringency makes them vulnerable, for it is preferable to cut experiments rather than operating programs that have longstanding clients and constituents. Furthermore, it is also natural for incoming decision makers to tamper with experiments that are under way to make them more relevant to their immediate concerns, even if that means that the experiments will not now address the questions they were originally designed to answer.

Relative to starting new programs without information, much evaluation must be considered a low-cost strategy. For example, even the high-cost social experiments such as those concerning income maintenance or housing allowances are much cheaper than actually putting such programs into place. Programs designed sequentially with adequate evaluation and/or experimental information will presumably have lower costs and be more efficient and effective than those designed in an ad hoc manner.

Chapter 11
Summary and Conclusions

I HAVE SPENT most of this book examining common strategies for making public decisions and the ways in which they work individually. I made some appraisals of their worth using the factors defined in chapter 2 as important in public policy making. The factors ranged from efficiency to timeliness to robustness. Now, looking across all the strategies, what can we say? My discussion of each strategy shows a surprising number of question marks, meaning that we really do not know a priori how it would perform on a particular factor. We seem to know the most about static efficiency. When it comes to producing innovation, timeliness, equity, or corrigibility, we know a lot less. Perhaps these things are intrinsically harder to understand, although we reward those who analyze efficiency the most, guaranteeing it gets the most thought. Our ignorance suggests we be wary whenever advocates start pushing one or another strategy as a cure to a problem. No strategy clearly dominates another on every factor. All problems cannot be addressed effectively with a single strategy, and some may be reasonable substitutes for one another.

No strategy is immune to failure or pitfalls. Even the most competent and careful decision makers and analysts should expect an encounter with them.[1] Certainly, bureaus are always threatening to fail because of their internal structure and criteria for success. Most bureaus capture their managers after a time, and even the best eventually burn out.

There seems little alternative to the hard work of appraising both the generic and specific properties of our strategies.

However, appraisal is not a skill taught in the standard policy science curriculum. Acquisition of technique constantly overwhelms questions about the appropriateness of the strategy. Nor will one find much case material on the art of appraisal.[2]

I believe that broad appraisals of strategies are important and feasible. There are many methods of doing them, and doing them well is more important than how they are done. Thinking through strategies with a list of criteria or factors, or scoring them on their expected performance may make a modest positive difference in our choices. Eighteen years of service as a public administrator have convinced me that obtaining modest positive differences is not a bad objective and one that is feasible.

Notes
References
Index

Notes

CHAPTER 1. INTRODUCTION

1. Appraising a strategy within some given political economy is analogous to the problem of appraising alternative economic systems. There is no generally agreed set of criteria or weights to judge their worth. The old debate about central planning versus market systems focused on the feasibility of reaching efficient resource allocations in a planned economy. Now there is debate over relative transactions and information costs and the effects of differential incentive systems. See Vickers (1983) for a discussion of overall judgments or "appreciations" as he calls them. See also Brewer and de Leon (1983).

2. Some literature suggests that bureaucrats may prefer a "quiet life" to aggrandizement of budget and staff. This may well be true. However, in the federal government, bureaus that publicly declare their desire for a quiet life are going to be in trouble with their sponsors and clients. Asking for the same real budget and staff each year violates well-established budgetary rules. So whatever federal managers may personally prefer, they cannot act as if they want the quiet life.

3. See Kelman (1981) for a discussion of reasons. For a general comparison of regulatory alternatives to market systems, see Mitnick (1980).

4. For an overview, see Johnson (1984) and Nelson (1984). For a recent critique of national economic planning, see Lavoie (1985).

5. For a historical description of patent trends, see National Science Board (1988)

6. Bator (1958) contains a comprehensive statement of market failure from the perspective of Paretian welfare economics. Later discussions of market failure emphasize institutional factors

175

more—for example, asymmetries in information, difficulties in constructing contracts and verifying compliance, transactions costs, etc. See Stiglitz (1986).

7. The supersonic transport is a famous example. During its development, it became clear that the aircraft would never break even. Actors with pure profit motivations would never have proceeded to deploy it. Since the British and French governments were involved, extra-market considerations were heavily involved, and the plane flew. As long as it continues to fly, it requires significant subsidies from Britain and France. See Morris and Hough (1987). Horwitch (1982) provides a history of U.S. development efforts. For a generally negative view of governments involved in commercial development projects, see Eads and Nelson (1971) and Office of Science and Technology Policy (1982).

8. See Nelson (1981).

9. Unintended or unanticipated consequences of well-intentioned policies frequently make a situation worse and sometimes irreversibly worse. For examples, see Hall (1982) and Sieber (1981).

10. Consider the 1985 Challenger disaster. Suppose that the Challenger had flown successfully, despite its well-documented past difficulties with its O-rings. The success would have validated the view that the system worked. So the risks NASA ran were acceptable or, at most, should have been reduced in the course of routine business. Given the actual failure, however, NASA's entire budget and structure is being overhauled. What's more, its belief system and "operational code" are being changed.

CHAPTER 2. APPRAISAL OF STRATEGIES

1. Janis (1989) observes that both public and private decision makers operate in different modes depending on the stakes and costs of decision making. He advocates "vigilant" decision making for really important decisions. Here one searches for alternatives and appraises them in a systematic way. In this book we are concerned with designing vigilant methods.

2. The form of appraisals and advice is variable. Questions can always be turned into criteria and vice versa. Breyer (1984), for example, uses "matching" criteria: he tries to see whether economic and social regulation are appropriately matched with the problems that brought them about. Not surprisingly, he finds poor matches in many cases and suggests alternatives that might be better.

3. In the federal government, many unwarranted strategies are turned back by demanding more information. This is especially effective when there is no experience with the strategy. Decision makers can then prudently demand rigorous demonstrations or experiments, knowing full well that it will be many years before results are in. By providing funds for demonstrations or experiments, decision makers buy off advocates by apparent willingness to act on positive evidence, and they mollify opponents by a willingness to wait for negative evidence. Of course, rigorous evidence, either positive or negative, rarely ever arrives.

4. One strain of policy science literature advocates that major policy decisions be made using more public participation (McCarthy, 1978). But extensive public participation increases the time required to arrive at decisions. Some now feasible strategies may become infeasible because there is no guarantee that increased participation will generate consensus rather than more conflict.

5. For the microeconomic view of the world, see, for example, Rhoads (1985) and Ward (1979).

6. See McCloskey (1983) and Nelson (1981) for discussions of what economists believe as opposed to what they can prove logically or empirically.

7. If an organization concentrates its command, control, and communications systems on becoming statically efficient, it, may, of course, forgo opportunities for dynamic efficiency, that is, maximizing long-run profits through the discovery and introduction of new products and processes. Schumpeter (1947) argued for organizational "slack" so that, when an opportunity for innovation came up, it could be seized. However, the justification of slack for these purposes to hard-headed businessmen and equity markets interested in high short-run returns is difficult.

8. Microeconomics frequently defines the economy as a whole as a single productive organization, even though there is no general manager for market economies. Economies can then be considered as statically efficient or inefficient, depending on their position relative to a global production possibility frontier.

9. The firm's problem is: max $\pi_T = \pi_A + \pi_B$ subject to $F(A,B) = 0$, the implicit equation for the production possibility frontier. A necessary condition for a maximum is that the price ratio equal the slope of the frontier, the marginal rate of transformation.

10. If we believe that there are interactions between an organization's design and "hard" production technology, then production possibility frontiers for firms and bureaus producing the same out-

puts may well have different shapes. See Murnane and Nelson (1984).

11. If we depart from a single-objective, neoclassical theory of the firm, and let the firm have multiple objectives, then firms begin to look and behave like bureaus.

12. Management experts believe that one of the reasons the United States has balance of payments difficulties is a loss of technological competitiveness. A combination of factors accounts for this—lack of technologically oriented managers, demands for short-run profits, and the inability to transform research into tangible products. Japanese industry, in contrast, is able to meet all of these conditions. See, for example, Hayes and Abernathy (1980).

13. See Usher (1964).

14. See Stiglitz (1986) for a discussion on this point.

15. For an overview of the innovation literature with respect to the private firm, see Kamien and Schwartz (1982) and Dosi (1988). For a recent comparison of the effects of R&D in monopolistic and competitive markets see Stiglitz (1986). Literature on innovation in bureaus is sparser, but see Lewis (1980) and Doig and Hargrove (1988).

16. In biology, evolution through natural selection is an invisible process. It adjusts species to their environment without anyone worrying about the adjustment, although we cannot say that some outcome is desired a priori.

17. This portrait has been overdone. Most bureaus can and do operate slowly. Most decisions are routine, and speed is not necessary in making them. While the phones may be ringing all the time in the White House or the Pentagon, most bureaus could be more relaxed, except for having to live up to the image of major decisions being made under intense time pressure. Through the design of their work, decision makers determine the time pressure they will suffer.

18. See Schulman (1975).

19. This assumes, of course, that an agency is interested in learning lessons and establishes the capability to do so.

20. See Gansler (1986) and Stubbing (1986).

21. See Nelkin (1971) for an account.

CHAPTER 3. THE ROLES OF MARKETS

1. Baumol (1952) and Bator (1958) present the standard cases of static market failure, but neither discusses the capability and will

of government to correct market failure. In recent years, the inability of government to perfect markets has been a major theme in economics and political science. See chapter 5.

2. Any political economy, of course, generates a large supply of declared market failures. To stakeholders, markets are failing all the time. Government always faces more failing markets than it can possibly correct. A distinction must also be made between market failure—where some barrier prevents prices from doing their job of allocation and signaling—and market success—where the market induces allocative and technical efficiency but there is political or social dislike of the outcome. In either case interest groups mobilize, and pressure for government action increases.

3. See Braudel (1979) for a detailed description of the economic functions of medieval fairs.

4. See Neuberger and Duffy (1976) for a discussion of transactions language.

5. Market failure resulting from imperfect information has been the subject of intense research in recent years. Given a lack of information or given asymmetrical information, some trades that would benefit both parties cannot be made (Akerlof, 1970; Kim, 1985). See Hayek (1945) for the classic statement on the role of information in the economy. For a general survey of the economics of information, see Hirschleifer and Reilly (1979).

6. Nothing, of course, prevents strategic political behavior designed to persuade the state to act in a way favorable to one's own interests. The implicit assumption is that either no trader has incentives or capability to engage in politics or that market structure cannot easily be changed through political means.

7. The existence, uniqueness, and stability of the competitive equilibrium have been majors topics of mathematical economics for the last fifty years. Under a standard, stylized set of assumptions, mathematical economists have demonstrated all three both in static and some dynamic models. See Weintraub (1985).

8. Some observers hold that firms mold consumer tastes and preferences through advertising. Informational advertising, letting consumers know prices and locations, is beneficial, but image-creating advertising is socially costly.

9. China has discovered that a market system requires some minimum infrastructure. For example, if a nation wants to encourage innovation using private markets, then some system that allows innovators to keep the returns from their efforts is necessary. As a result, China has recently established a patent system.

10. For an institutional view of the rise of markets, see Mockyr

(1985), North (1981), and Rosenberg and Birdzell (1986). See Finley (1985) for a description of a classical economy.

11. There is, of course, interaction between political systems and economic systems. See Usher (1981). Hirschman (1977) argues that shifts to markets helped control political "passions."

12. The literature on the Industrial Revolution is very large, since it was a pivotal event for Western political economy. For a recent overview, see Mockyr (1985).

13. A general competitive equilibrium exists when (1) every household and every firm is in equilibrium, (2) all markets clear, and (3) every firm earns zero profit. For more technical discussion, see Quirk and Saposnick (1968).

14. More detailed descriptions of this process can be found in any microeconomics textbook. There are some standard conditions and restrictions that have to hold to reach equilibrium and to move from one to the other. For an appraisal of general equilibrium theory, see Weintraub (1985).

15. A substantial literature exists on how the pursuit of private interests by organized political pressure groups retards static and dynamic efficiency. See Olson (1965, 1982).

16. As was noted in chapter 2, Pareto efficiency is the economist's preferred welfare criterion. Economists remain attached to this principle because they believe it is weak enough for large numbers of people to subscribe to it. The intense debate in recent years over the welfare criteria proposed by Rawls and others since the 1970s suggests that this may not be the case. See Rawls (1971). In any case, Pareto efficiency is intimately connected with perfectly competitive markets through the two basic theorems of welfare economics.

17. The second basic theorem of welfare economics states that if consumers have convex indifference maps and firms have convex production sets; if there are comprehensive markets for all goods and services; if there is perfect information; and if government can make costless lump-sum transfers, then some set of prices exists that will achieve any desired Pareto-efficient allocation. See Boadway and Bruce (1984).

18. Schumpeter (1947). See Nelson and Winter (1982) for a review of the literature on the various Schumpeterian hypotheses.

19. Economists influenced by the Austrian tradition emphasize that market processes are more important than equilibrium states. It is the search for profit that drives entrepreneurs. See Kirzner (1973, 1979).

20. Keeping track of scientific and technical information implies that firms need some ability to process information flowing from science and engineering and some R&D capability of their own.

21. Congealing is sometimes portrayed as a linear process from basic and applied research to development, test, and evaluation and then to market. In fact, there are loops and interconnections between the stages. See Rosenberg (1982).

22. There is a difference in perspective between economists and management scientists. Economists tend to emphasize demand factors as calling innovations into existence. Management scientists tend to argue that firms ought to be using technology to create new products for which demand can be generated. Failure to do so decreases the market shares of a firm and the economic competitiveness of a country.

23. Some economists believe that major innovations come clustered together. Their joint impact creates "long waves" of growth and development. See Freeman (1982) and Mensch (1979).

24. See Stiglitz (1986) and Stoneman (1983) on this point.

25. Coase (1974) argues that the lighthouse example was never very well taken, since lighthouses were privately operated in England.

26. See Nelson (1984).

27. Economics defines two kinds of externalities: technological and pecuniary. Technological ones impact production and consumption but are not mediated by a price; pecuniary ones change prices. The former may need policy correction, but not the latter. The economy adjusts to changed prices, whatever their cause.

28. See Schelling (1983).

29. See Akerlof (1970), Kim (1985), and Phlips (1988).

30. See Coase (1960).

31. The work of Mansfield, Romeo, and Wagner (1979) on social and private returns from innovation suggests some hiding hand principle. If, ex ante, managers knew the true ex post private returns to many innovations, they would never undertake them.

32. Japanese managers and firms are said to be more oriented to longer-run returns.

33. See Dasgupta and Stiglitz (1980) and Stoneman (1983).

34. See Averch (1985) for a discussion of civilian technology policy.

35. See Barzel (1968).

36. See Cheung (1973).

37. Policy designers will not ordinarily suggest setting up a market with a monopoly supplier to solve a problem.

CHAPTER 4. THE MICROECONOMICS OF BUREAUS

1. Bureaucratic failure has been a prominent theme in recent policy analysis. See Dryzek (1983), Hanusch (1983), Hogwood and Peters (1985), Pierce (1981), Wilson (1989), and Wolf (1988).

2. See Selznick (1949) and Kaufman (1960) for portraits of competent bureaus. Sayles and Chandler (1971) believed that NASA had discovered effective procedures for managing complex, large-scale projects. Recently, the Office of Personnel Management began reporting on excellent federal bureaus.

3. Economists assign investments in bureaucratic activity as one of the reasons why growth in U.S. productivity has been so low in recent years. See, for example, Dumas (1986) and Wolff (1987).

4. See Sapolsky (1972) and Sayles and Chandler (1971). The systems approach NASA had developed was supposed to guard against technological dangers and risks, but the 1986 shuttle disaster suggests that the approach was not sufficient to prevent failure.

5. See Stubbing (1986) and Gansler (1986). Peck and Scherer (1962) is a classic investigation of the weapons procurement process and its difficulties.

6. Recent and extensive overviews of the privatization debate can be found in Donahue (1989) and Pack (1989).

7. In the very short run, politicking and feuding seem the most important thing in the life of a bureau. But after a few months no one other than participants and historians remembers what the issues were or who won, and even they have difficulty. In contrast, if bureaus, say, are powerfully motivated by the size of their budgets or the growth rate, then their strategies, inputs, and outputs are all permanently affected. To say that bureaus are motivated means, of course, that their structure and incentive systems have been designed or have evolved to make individual bureaucrats act as if these things mattered.

8. Most of the modeling work has been done on bureaus that deliver goods and services. Models of regulatory bureaus are rarer, but see Bendor and Moe (1985).

9. If we remove an a priori preference for a market system, two more justifications are possible—changing a market economy to a

more centrally planned one and realizing the targets of some central plan. See Rees (1984).

10. The market failure case for government economic activity can be found in Baumol (1952), Bator (1958), Boadway and Bruce (1984), and Stiglitz (1986). Baumol (1984) discusses the alternatives to public supply.

11. Actually, the Labor government nationalized the "commanding heights" of the economy, including transportation, energy, health, and the Bank of England. See the chart in Gardner (1988, p. 115).

12. See Dery (1984) on the ways in which decision makers, analysts, and the public define problems and needs.

13. See Nelkin (1971) for an example in housing. In the 1960s the Kennedy administration wanted to provide R&D subsidies to the housing industry. It felt that housing output was too low and that the construction industry was unaware of technological possibilities. The administration also believed that aircraft technology could be used to build houses faster. However, firms in the housing industry itself, as well as construction unions and local zoning officials, objected.

14. For an historic overview of the Interstate Commerce Commission, see Gujarati (1984). The commission achieved control of surface transportation, but did not gain jurisdiction over the airlines.

15. See Titmuss (1971).

16. Elkin (1986) makes an interesting international comparison of regulatory frameworks. He contrasts the American concern with efficiency with British concern with political and social implications of regulation. See also Rhoads (1985).

17. Depending on their organizational level, bureaus will encounter many sponsors. Legislatures or their committees are frequently defined as sponsors. Major departments have to aggregate and coordinate requests from constituent bureaus. Each department has to persuade the OMB that its budget submission is worthy. OMB and nominally the president expect departments to defend the budget they approve before Congress. There are at least six sponsors in the Congress—two authorizing committees, two appropriations committees, and two budget committees, all of which have to approve a bureau's budget. Obviously, there is much room for multilateral strategic behavior.

18. The bureau has a constrained maximization problem, max $B(Q)$ subject to $B(Q) \geq C(Q)$. Assuming the constraint is effective,

the bureau's equilibrium output Q^* is given by the solution of the two equations:

$$B'(Q) = (\mu/\mu+1) \, C'(Q)$$

$$B(Q) = C(Q)$$

where μ is a Lagrange multiplier (Chiang, 1984). The feasible values for μ are $\mu < -1$ and $\mu > 0$. If $-1 < \mu < 0$, marginal budget will be negative, and so the budget-maximizing bureau will not operate there. For $\mu < -1$, marginal budget is greater than marginal cost, and the bureau can increase its budget by expanding output. For $\mu > 0$, marginal budget is less than the marginal cost of the output.

19. See Conybeare (1984) and Miller and Moe (1983) for detailed expositions of this model.

20. Perceived lack of team play also generates punishment in private sector organizations.

21. Miller and Moe (1983).

22. See Savas (1987) for arguments in favor of privatization.

23. See Wildavsky (1979) for a catalogue of these strategies.

24. Bendor, Taylor, and Van Gaalen (1985).

25. A risk-averse bureau is defined as one having a concave utility function. In the case here, the utility function is the expected budget. So it should be written as $U[E(B)] > E[U(B)]$.

26. Bureaucratic reform follows its own cycle. Initially effective reforms eventually lose their effectiveness. Organizational memory fades, and those with a stake in reform move on. Eventually, reforms are seen as themselves in need of reform, since they get in the way of achieving some objectives that a bureau currently believes important. For example, the Central Intelligence Agency's penchant for covert action has been reformed and constrained many times, but covert action has always returned in one form or another as a major activity of the agency.

27. For example, Bendor and Moe (1985).

28. For descriptions of this defense supplier network and how it works, see Gansler (1986) and Stubbing (1986).

29. Of course, there is a strain of business literature that deals with burnt-out firms and executives.

30. Neither Doig and Hargrove (1988) nor Lewis (1980) discusses public innovations that failed and whether the same conditions held.

CHAPTER 5. BUREAUCRATIC FAILURE

1. As was noted in chapter 4, there is a growing literature on failure. However, each author approaches failure with a different perspective, and there is no canonical theory of failure in bureaus as there is for failure in markets.

2. See Allen (1988) on the need to ignore sunk costs in the private sector. See Wolf (1969) and Behn (1981).

3. The single largest horror story in recent years is the Challenger disaster. However, nearly all NASA participants went by the book, the collected folk wisdom and standard procedures that had been worked out over the years. That this book might have had a restricted range of application was never an admissible possibility. See Presidential Commission on the Space Shuttle Challenger Disaster (1986).

4. Competition in the private sector is clearly not sufficient to control perverse behavior. Firms as diverse as Ford, the Pennsylvania Railroad, USX, and Bank of America have all engaged in behavior that was damaging to themselves.

5. Simon's entire body of work reflects this doubt and describes ways to compensate. See Nelson and Winter (1982) and Williamson (1985).

6. See Murnane and Nelson (1984).

7. One standard example in the economics literature compares the efficiency of publicly owned airlines (Australia). See Davies (1971). Another standard example concerns solid waste disposal. See Savas (1987).

8. Depending on contract procedures, budgets need not be expended in the same fiscal year they were authorized and appropriated. However, they can be obligated for expenditures in future years.

9. See Sayles and Chandler (1971) and Sapolsky (1972).

10. See Haveman (1987) for an account of the War on Poverty.

11. For an account of how the military services captured PPBS, see Rosen (1987).

CHAPTER 6. REGULATION

1. Social regulation refers to rules and standards applied to entire industries to meet environmental, health, or safety con-

cerns. There is no presumption that these industries have natural monopoly characteristics as would be true of most economic regulation. Traditionally, economic regulation constrains prices and entry.

2. Postal and railway service are completely publicly provided in most Western European counties. Telecommunications, gas, and airlines are predominately public. Public ownership of significant steel and shipbuilding capacity is common in a number of countries. See Petersen (1985, p. 393), for precise distributions of public and private ownership in Western Europe.

3. See Ozaki (1984).

4. See Goldman (1977).

5. See Mills and Graves (1986).

6. See Petersen (1985) for background on these agencies.

7. See Denison (1979).

8. Economists argued that, despite some unfortunate transaction costs, the effects of deregulation have been positive (Bailey 1986).

9. See R. Posner (1975) for an overview.

10. See Stigler (1971) and Peltzman (1976).

11. By 1985 the budget of the Interstate Commerce Commission was half what it had been in 1980. There was no real growth in government regulatory activity if measured by total dollars expended. See Weiss and Klass (1986).

12. Ramsey prices are the set that result when a natural monopoly is instructed to maximize social welfare under a break-even constraint. The percentage deviation from marginal cost should be inversely proportional to the elasticity of demand. In the case of one good, the formulation is $P(Q)-MC(Q)/P(Q) = -(k/k+1)\times(1/\eta)$ where k is the so-called Ramsey number and η is elasticity. For a derivation, see Crew and Kleindorfer (1986).

13. See Eads (1982) for an account.

14. Contestability theory argues that under a set of more or less plausible conditions—especially costless entry and exit—natural monopolists will be deterred from exploiting their positions. See Baumol, Panzar, and Willig (1982) for a discussion of contestability theory. For a critique, see Shepherd (1984).

15. See Weiss and Klass (1986) for an account of deregulation movements in different industries. See Crew and Rowley (1986) for a stab at theory. See Mitnick (1980, chap. 9).

16. See Sharkey (1982) for an intellectual history of the natural monopoly concept. Sharkey notes that for a multiproduct firm a

natural monopoly must exhibit both economies of scale and economies of scope. Economies of scope refer to cases were joint production of two or more outputs is less costly than the combined costs of producing the same outputs by two or more independent firms. Economies of scope may arise from indivisible inputs used for one product that become freely available for producing another output.

17. However, in traditional analysis, natural monopolies were believed to be technically efficient, that is, they always produced whatever output they chose at least cost. Some literature suggests that monopolists may work hard at bolstering their positions, occurring unnecessary costs. See Cowling and Mueller (1978).

18. Since Harberger (1954) first estimated the total loss resulting from allocative inefficiency as .1 percent of GNP, there has been a lengthy dispute on its exact magnitude. Curing inefficiency is the economist's stock in trade. Therefore much effort has gone into showing that the true figure is much larger than Harberger's.

19. Crew and Kleindorfer (1986) identify five alternatives: regulation, public enterprise, franchise bidding, contracting, and deregulation. Williamson (1985) presents a lengthy discussion of franchise bidding as an institution. Franchise bidding involves public auction of the right to function as a protected monopolist. Few policy makers or economists consider bidding a practical alternative. There are problems of constructing and judging competing contracts, of administrative complexity, and of cost. Public contracting raises the kinds of bureaucratic issues discussed in chapter 3. Nor does contracting necessarily achieve satisfactory delivery of previously public goods.

20. The Justice Department filed suit against IBM in 1969 and had it dismissed in 1982. Each side had incentives to increase the time taken for acquisition of information. See Petersen (1985). In the 1970s Posner estimated that 30 percent of the cases took six years.

21. See Bos (1986) and Rees (1984) for a discussion of publicly owned firms. See Petersen (1985) for discussion of the United States' experience.

22. Rees (1984) notes that formal theory suggests that public enterprises will show low labor productivity and excessive labor intensity. He suggests that lack of property rights in bureaus as compared to firms causes inefficiency. Taxpayers cannot hold bureaus accountable for performance the way shareholders of a firm can.

23. Murphy and Soyster (1982).

24. See Westfield (1970) and Magat (1976).

25. A production function is homothetic if it is a monotonic (order-preserving) transformation of a homogeneous production function. Let $Q = F(K,L)$ be homogeneous of degree r. Let $Q' = G(Q)$ and $dQ'/dQ > 0$. Then Q' is homothetic.

26. See Kelman (1981) for a discussion of ethical objections to market-type solutions for environmental problems.

27. See Hill and Utterback (1979).

28. See Denison (1983).

29. See Grabowski (1976) and Grabowski and Vernon (1983).

30. See Klevorick (1971).

31. See Besanko (1987).

32. European philosophers often advocate intense public participation in decision making. Regulatory hearings may be a proximate example of public participation in decision making. But substantively it is not clear whether the process truly enhances performance.

33. See Breyer (1984) for more extensive discussion on this point.

34. See Baron and Meyerson (1982) and Taylor (1984).

CHAPTER 7. PLANNING AND BUDGETING SYSTEMS

1. See Mikesell (1986) for discussion and an example.

2. See Mosher (1979) for a history of OMB and a comparison with the General Accounting Office.

3. PPBS as practiced in the Defense Department was the product of Rand Corporation economists and was codified in Hitch and McKean (1960). A number of Rand staff joined McNamara to put PPBS in place. The interactions of the analysts with the military created a new folklore and craft wisdom about the uses and abuses of analytical approaches to complex questions. See Enthoven and Smith (1971) for an early 1970s view.

4. There are many accounts of the birth and death of PPBS. One view holds that it was a good thing to try and that it failed because of a recalcitrant bureaucracy. Another strain holds that it was fundamentally flawed procedure because it required capabilities that bureaus could never have. See Schick (1973) and Wildavsky (1966).

5. President Nixon changed the name of the Budget Bureau to the Office of Management and Budget. No president since has tried to change the name back, although the emphasis on management has varied.

6. ZBB was invented in the private sector but first applied

mainly to organizations that had measurable output. See Phyrr (1973). By the time Carter entered the White House, there existed a number of evaluations showing that ZBB had not been very effective in Georgia. But there is no evidence that Carter or his staff read these evaluations or, if they did, used them. Certainly the scale of ZBB required in the federal establishment should have signaled a close examination of the benefits and costs. However, incoming presidents like to recreate past environments that made them comfortable, whether or not these environments are relevant to current circumstances. See Lauth (1978) for a discussion of ZBB in Georgia state government during Carter's time.

7. Of course, once a bureau knows it will, in fact, receive a lower budget, it will usually want to reorder its packages or disaggregate them and rank differently.

8. Federal bureaus consider cuts of 10 percent to be serious, and they consider cuts of 20 percent to be disastrous. They have an entire repertoire of responses to avert such outcomes. See Wildavsky (1979).

9. Stockman (1986).

10. Wildavsky has always argued that these economically rational formats and procedures are politically irrational. They remove choice from elected officials, increase conflict, and are incorrigible on the discovery of error. See Wildavsky (1979).

CHAPTER 8. BENEFIT-COST ANALYSIS

1. See Feldman (1989) for a view of analysis processes as markets for ideas.

2. Somewhat ironically, as environmental, health, and safety (EHS) regulations spread, it became necessary to estimate their benefits and costs, to regulate the regulators by requiring them to produce estimates of the indirect impacts of regulation on productivity and competitiveness. Regulators were "suboptimized" on their own objectives. In the early 1970s there were then no processes or institutions to force them to consider overall social benefits and costs.

3. Some writers restrict the term BCA only to those cases where all benefits and costs of policies or actions can be expressed in discounted monetary terms.

4. The rules for such mergers have yet to be developed. See Majone and Quade (1980) and Quade and Miser (1985).

5. See Dupuit (1969).

6. See Federal Inter-Agency River Basin Committee (1950).

7. See, for example, Eckstein (1958), McKean (1958), Krutilla and Eckstein (1958), and Maas (1962).

8. See any modern text in operations research, for example, Hillier and Lieberman (1980).

9. Defining alternatives is not a trivial task. One of the major justifications of BCA is that it may generate new problem definitions and alternatives superior to the ones that decision makers begin with. See Dery (1984) on definition of problems.

10. Competitive market systems price alternatives at their true social cost. But most often alternatives of concern to BCA are not evaluated by markets, or if they are, they are evaluated imperfectly.

11. The procedures for revealing effects or outcomes is supposed to be appropriate to the problem at hand and may range from "back of the envelope" curve drawing to large-scale analytical models or simulations. There are two formal model building schools. One prefers general-purpose models that can answer many questions. The other believes that models should be tailored to particular problems with the salient variables identified by theory or empirical evidence. Large, general-purpose models have more scope and do not have to be modified for every new question. The small, sharply focused ones have more resolution and are easier to understand. For a discussion of modeling, see Quade and Miser (1985).

12. An alternative criterion is ratio of benefits to costs is given by $\Sigma\ B_{it}/(1+r)^t/\Sigma\ C_{it}/(1+r)^t$. If the ratio is greater than one, projects should be selected; if less than one, projects should not be selected.

13. The decision maker in this case can make selections in stages. First, any and all projects with negative net present benefits can be eliminated from further consideration—project 6. Then, from among the remaining projects, one can choose, in descending order, the ones with the highest positive net benefit per dollar up to the point where budget is exhausted.

14. Consumers' surplus has one of the most checkered histories of all microeconomic concepts. Economists would prefer changes in aggregate utility engendered by public activities as the true measure of benefits. But this is notoriously difficult to get. Consequently, some substitute for these changes must be found. So they try to compute the money equivalents of changes in utility. These equivalents will be an imperfect measure except under very special circumstances. For an overview of the consumers' surplus debate, see Morey (1984).

15. Any modern econometrics text covers the necessary proce-

dures for identifying and estimating demand curves. See Wonnacott and Wonnacott (1979), for example.

16. See Willig (1976), Hausman (1981), and Morey (1984).

17. The interagency coordinating committee is a popular mechanism at the federal level. Here technical staff and administrators try to exchange sufficient information to coordinate their activities voluntarily. As might be expected, such committees become a forum for the pursuit of individual agency objectives. The interagency "czar" is another alternative. For example, the United States now has a czar to coordinate programs to fight drug problems.

18. See Ray (1984) for a list.

19. This discussion follows Pearce (1983).

20. Presidential Commission on the Space Shuttle Challenger Accident (1986).

21. See Presidential Commission on Three Mile Island (1979).

22. Differential outcomes should track with differences in real-world outcomes and not be attributable to capricious settings of model parameters. One can usually make some a priori analysis come out in any direction one desires, no matter the situation that would occur were alternatives to be tested by actual implementation. Usually one tries to obtain a proper calibration by varying assumptions and parameter estimates against some known, perhaps historical base case. Models may not be sensitive enough to discern differences. Some factor that is very important in reality may only be treated sketchily in a model.

CHAPTER 9. COST-EFFECTIVENESS AND SYSTEMS ANALYSIS

1. *Systems analysis* is a term with many meanings, especially in the computer field. Here it means the systematic exploration and comparison of alternative strategies, budgets, and technologies for reaching public objectives. See Quade and Miser (1985).

2. The literature makes a distinction between uncertainty where probabilities of outcome can be estimated and ignorance where not enough experience exists to make estimates.

3. Prior to this substantive sensitivity analysis, a good deal of work is necessary on the calibration of models or simulations. Parameters of the model have to be set to represent the real world adequately. Differences in outcomes or the lack of difference cannot reasonably be attributed to the models being used.

4. For background, see Brzezinski (1986), Drell, Farley, and Hol-

loway (1985), Guerier and Thompson (1987), and Office of Technology Assessment (1988).

5. The U.S. curve is drawn above the one for the USSR because the United States is much more densely populated.

6. See, for example, Union of Concerned Scientists (1984).

7. Argument over SDI has been a growth industry. For background, see Office of Technology Assessment (1988).

8. Since BCAs absorb scarce resources, they need to be well designed and elicit maximum information for given cost. Literature critical of BCA approaches to decision making is extensive. See, for example, Tribe (1973) and Baram (1980).

9. The critical literature is very large. See, for example, Baram (1980).

CHAPTER 10. DEMONSTRATION, EXPERIMENT, AND EVALUATION

1. Randomized treatments are ideal from a technical or scientific perspective, but they are difficult to achieve in practice. Consequently, much of the theory of evaluation consists of finding reasonable or appropriate substitutes for randomization and of estimating impacts from nonrandom procedures. The classic work on this subject is Campbell and Stanley (1966). See also Rossi and Freeman (1982).

2. Experiments, however, have to be defined properly relative to the salient policy question. The original design of the negative income tax did not include any treatment requiring work by recipients. As political debate continued, it was clear that such a requirement would be necessary for any to program to pass, but there would be no evidence on it. No new experiment on the most salient treatment could be mounted in time. See Greenberg and Robins (1985) for an account.

3. The literature focuses on technical pitfalls that can lead to poor practice. One can design bad survey instruments or have invalid measures. But these are easy to fix or avoid. See Hatry (1980) for a list of fixable pitfalls.

4. See Averch (1987b) for an account of the factors that influence applied social science demand and supply. See Alchon (1985) and Lyons (1969) for an account of social science in this period. For a history of social program evaluation, see Madaus, Stufflebeam, and Scriven (1987).

5. Airasian (1987) observes that 1960s-style social programs assumed that government programs could change individual behavior. Earlier programs, in contrast, assumed there was nothing wrong with individuals per se. Individual difficulties arose resulted from the unintended consequences of social change. Thus, redistribution and maintenance were necessary, not the transformation of individuals.

6. Evaluations are frequently divided into two types: formative and summative. Formative evaluations are designed to provide information in time to improve the operations of a program. Summative evaluations are designed to determine end impacts or results. In principle, they are supposed to occur after all the lessons of formative evaluations have been absorbed and implemented, that is, they are supposed to be applied to programs optimized through formative evaluations. Of course, this principle is often violated in practice. Hence critics of a negative summative evaluation argue that, if only the program had been optimized, the evaluation would have been positive.

7. Campbell (1969) argued for an "experimenting society." Rivlin (1971) argued that the benefits of a systematic experimental strategy would outweigh the costs, because only experiments would reveal effective alternatives.

8. See Greenberg and Robins (1985), who note that the abundant technical evidence generates methodological controversy that prevents program application. They suggest that policies and programs for which there is minimal evidence about efficiency and effectiveness are more likely to be enacted.

9. Any proposed experiments involved testing market devices for problem solving. Thus, educational and housing voucher experiments were proposed that would give recipients greater impact in the market. Inefficient and ineffective bureaucratic services to the poor could be abolished, since the poor knew better than bureaucrats what they needed. It was only their lack of market power that prevented them from getting what they needed.

10. There will be far more nominal purposes than real purposes. To obtain political support for a bill, sponsors often claim their program will assist in solving a huge number of problems. In the late 1980s, for example, federal agencies justify budget requests by claiming to solve problems of international competitiveness. If the greenhouse effect pans out, then programs will be justified by showing how they reduce greenhouse problems. Technically, the more objectives a program serves, the more difficult it is to design.

11. See Patton and Sawicki (1986) for a description of research designs where true random experiments are not possible. Most approaches follow the guidelines laid down in Campbell and Stanley (1966).

12. This kind of problem arises frequently in clinical medical trials. Today, for example, there is enormous short-run pressure to make the drug AZT available to all who have AIDS or who test positively for its virus. However, the long-term effects of AZT are unknown.

13. Evaluators sometimes say lessons can be derived from formative evaluations designed to improve the program. Summative evaluations then estimate the impact of an optimized program. From a policy perspective, however, the consequences of formative evaluations are about the same as summative evaluations. Critical formative evaluations raise the same issues as summative ones despite assurances that decision makers and sponsors are willing to hold off judgments.

14. See Collingridge and Reeves (1986).

15. There is the possibility of designing sequential experiments or demonstrations that produce valid, partial information at various points in time. Technically, this is difficult to accomplish and a consequence may be the early use of erroneous partial information that preempts the final results from having any significance.

16. This is the justification used when the utility of evaluations and experiments become an issue. Whether this is a cost-effective way of changing public debate compared to other means is problematic.

CHAPTER 11. SUMMARY AND CONCLUSIONS

1. Janis (1989) lays out some recommended practices for high-quality "vigilant" decision making. These involve raising questions and reviewing at each step in the decision process. However, he neglects the innate propensity for failure that at least our public strategies have.

2. An examination of recent texts on policy analysis shows that their main content is analytical technique, primarily benefit-cost analysis with a smattering of evaluation and planning technique. See, for example, Patton and Sawicki (1986) and Stokey and Zeckhauser (1978). Weimer and Aidan (1989) appraise markets and bureaus. Compare all of these to Vickers (1983).

References

Airasian, P. W. 1987. "Societal Experimentation." In *Evaluation Models: Viewpoints on Education and Services Evaluation*, ed. G. F. Madaus, M. S. Scriven, and D. L. Stufflebeam. Boston: Kluwer Nijhoff.

Akerlof, G. 1970. "The Market for Lemons." *Quarterly Journal of Economics* 84:488–500. The classic article on market failure when there is asymmetric information and parties cannot improve their knowledge or modify their institutions.

Alchon, G. 1985. *The Invisible Hand of Planning: Capitalism, Social Science, and the State in the 1920's.* Princeton, N.J.: Princeton University Press.

Allen, B. T. 1988. *Managerial Economics.* New York: Harper and Row.

Apgar, W. C., and H. J. Brown. 1987. *Microeconomics and Public Policy.* Glenview, Ill.: Scott, Foresman.

Asch, P. and R. Seneca. 1985. *Government and the Marketplace.* New York: Dryden Press.

Averch, H. A. 1985. *A Strategic Analysis of Science and Technology Policy.* Baltimore: Johns Hopkins University Press.

———. 1987a. "The Averch-Johnson (A-J) Effect" In *The New Palgrave*, ed. J. Eatwell, M. Millgate, and P. Newman. New York: Stockton Press.

———. 1987b. "Applied Social Science, Policy Science, and the Federal Government." *Knowledge* 8:521–44.

Bailey, E. E. 1986. "Price and Productivity Change Following Regulation: The U.S. Experience." *Economic Journal* 96:1–17.

Bailey, E. E., ed. 1988. *Public Regulation: New Perspectives on Institutions and Policies.* Cambridge, Mass.: MIT Press. Contains several good surveys on recent developments in regulatory theory, one by Sappington and Stiglitz on information and regulation, one by Breyer on current legal issues, and one by Romer and Rosenthal on political models of regulation.

Baram, M. 1980. "Cost-Benefit Analysis: An Inadequate Basis for Health, Safety, and Environmental Regulatory Decision-making." *Ecology Law Quarterly* 8:473–531. Argues that traditional benefit-cost analysis ignores values and and legal issues that vitiate its use as a decision making process.

Bardach, E., and R. A. Kagan. 1982. *Social Regulation: Strategies for Reform.* New Brunswick, N.J.: Transaction Books.

Baron, D. P., and R. Meyerson. 1982. "Regulating a Monopolist with Unknown Costs." *Econometrica* 50:911–30. An important article on how to regulate firms when their costs are unknown to the regulator. Suggests incentives that reduce a firm's propensity to misrepresent its cost curves to the regulator.

Barzel, Y. 1968. "Optimal Timing of Innovation." *Review of Economics and Statistics* 50:348–55.

Bator, F. 1957. "The Simple Analytics of Welfare Maximization." *American Economic Review* 47:22–59. A simple, parsimonious exposition of optimal welfare principles as economists traditionally see them.

———. 1958. "The Anatomy of Market Failure." *Quarterly Journal of Economics* 72:351–79. A good companion piece to Bator (1957). Clear exposition of static market failures as defined in neoclassical economics.

Baumol, W. J. 1952. *Welfare Economics and the Theory of the State.* Cambridge, Mass.: Harvard University Press. An excellent survey of neoclassical economic justifications of state policy action.

———. 1984. "Toward a Theory of Public Enterprise." *Atlantic Economic Journal* 12:13–20.

Baumol, W. J., and A. Klevorick. 1970. "Input Choices and Rate-of—Return Regulation: An Overview of the Discussion." *Bell Journal of Economics and Management Science* 1:162–90. Remains the best single summary of the theory of rate-of-return regulation. Still very good on the basics.

Baumol, W. J., and W. E. Oates. 1979. *Economics, Environmental Policy, and the Quality of Life.* Englewood Cliffs, N.J.: Prentice-Hall.

Baumol, W. J., and W. E. Oates. 1988. *The Theory of Environmental Policy.* 2d ed. Cambridge: Cambridge University Press.

Baumol, W. J., J. Panzar, and R. Willig. 1982. *Contestable Markets and the Theory of Industry Structure.* New York. Harcourt Brace Jovanovich.

Behn, R. D. 1981. "Policy Analysis and Policy Politics." *Policy Analysis* 7:199–226.

Bendor, J., and T. M. Moe. 1985. "An Adaptive Model of Bureaucratic Politics." *American Political Science Review* 79:755–69.

Bendor, J., S. Taylor, and R. Van Gaalen. 1985. "Bureaucratic Expertise versus Legislative Authority: A Model of Deception and Monitoring in Budgeting." *American Political Science Review* 79:1041–59. Shows that bureaus can be controlled given sufficient information and monitoring skills. Contains simple but revealing models of bureaucratic behavior under various reporting schemes.

Berg, S., and J. Tschirhart. 1988. *Natural Monopoly Regulation.* Cambridge: Cambridge University Press.

Besanko, D. 1987. "Performance Versus Design Standards in the Regulation of Pollution." *Journal of Public Economics* 34:19–49.

Besanko, D., and D.E.M. Sappington. 1987. *Designing Regulatory Policy with Limited Information.* New York: Harwood Academic Publishers. A survey of recent developments in regulatory modeling where the traditional assumption of perfect demand and cost information held by the regulator is relaxed.

Boadway, R. W., and Bruce, N. 1984. *Welfare Economics.* New York: Basil Blackwell.

Bobrow, D., and J. S. Dryzek. 1987. *Policy Analysis by Design.* Pittsburgh, Pa.: University of Pittsburgh Press. A readable description of the various schools or styles of policy analysis.

Bos, D. 1986. *Public Enterprise Economics.* New York: North Holland.

Boudreaux, D., and R. B. Ekelund, Jr. 1987. "Regulation as an Exogenous Response to Market Failure: A Neo-Schumpeterian Response." *Journal of Institutional and Theoretical Economics* 143:537–54.

Braudel, F. 1979. *The Wheels of Commerce.* New York: Harper & Row.

Breton, A., and R. Weintrobe. 1982. *The Logic of Bureaucratic Conduct.* Cambridge: Cambridge University Press.

Brewer, G., and P. de Leon. 1983. *Foundations of Policy Analysis.* Homewood, Ill.: Dorsey Press.

Breyer, S. 1984. *Regulation*. Cambridge, Mass.: Harvard University Press. Tries to deduce the optimal form of regulation from the nature and structure of particular regulatory problems.

Brzezinski, Z., ed. 1986. *Promise or Peril: The Strategic Defensive Initiative*. Washington, D.C.: Ethics and Public Policy Center.

Campbell, D. E. 1987. *Resource Allocation Mechanisms*. Cambridge: Cambridge University Press. A good summary of the mechanism design literature as it relates to perfectly competitive market systems, although the criteria for a "good" mechanism offered by this literature are fairly remote from those that would be salient to decision makers.

Campbell, D. T. 1969. "Reforms as Experiments." *American Psychologist* 24:409–29. Argues optimistically for an experimenting society. An important statement by an advocate of social experiments. However, it does not show great awareness of actual decision-making processes and the role of evidence and analysis in these.

Campbell, D. T., and J. C. Stanley. 1966. *Experimental and Quasi—Experimental Designs for Research*. Chicago: Rand McNally.

Cheung, S. N. 1973. "The Fable of the Bees: An Economic Investigation." *Journal of Law and Economics* 16:11–33.

Chiang, A. C. 1984. *Fundamental Methods of Mathematical Economics*. 3d ed. New York: McGraw-Hill.

Clark, T. B., M. H. Kosters, and J. C. Miller III, eds. 1980. *Reforming Regulation*. Washington, D.C.: American Enterprise Institute for Public Policy Research.

Coase, R. 1960. "The Problem of Social Cost." *Journal of Law and Economics* 3:1–33.

———. 1974. "The Lighthouse in Economics." *Journal of Law and Economics* 17:457-76.

Collingridge, D. 1980. *The Social Control of Technology*. Milton Keynes, U.K.: Open University Press.

———. 1983. *Technology in the Policy Process*. New York: St. Martin's Press.

Collingridge, D., and C. Reeves. 1986. *Science Speaks to Power: The Role of Experts in Policymaking*. New York: St. Martin's Press.

Conybeare, J.A.C. 1984. "Bureaucracy, Monopoly, and Competition: A Critical Analysis of the Budget-Maximizing Model." *American Journal of Political Science* 28:479–502.

Cornes, R., and T. Sandler. 1986. *The Theory of Externalities, Pub-*

lic Goods, and Club Goods. Cambridge: Cambridge University Press.

Cowen, T. 1988. The Theory of Market Failure. Fairfax, Va.: George Mason University Press.

Cowling, K., and D. C. Mueller. 1978. "The Social Cost of Monopoly Power." Economic Journal 88:727–48.

Crane, J. A. 1982. The Evaluation of Social Policies. Boston: Kluwer Nijhoff.

Crew, M. A., ed. 1979. Policies in Public Utility Economics and Regulation. Boston: Lexington Books.

Crew, M. A., and P. R. Kleindorfer. 1986. The Economics of Public Utility Regulation. Cambridge, Mass.: MIT Press.

Crew, M. A., and C. K. Rowley. 1986. "Deregulation as an Instrument of Industrial Policy." Journal of Institutional and Theoretical Economics 142:52–71.

Cronbach, L. 1982. Designing Evaluations of Educational and Social Programs. San Francisco: Jossey-Bass.

Daneke, G. A., and D. J. Lemak, eds. 1985. Regulatory Reform Reconsidered. Boulder, Colo.: Westview Press.

Dasgupta, P., and J. Stiglitz. 1980. "Uncertainty, Industrial Structure and the Speed of R&D." Bell Journal of Economics and Management Science 11:1–28.

Davies, D. 1971. "The Efficiency of Public Versus Private Firms: The Case of Australia's Two Airlines." Journal of Law and Economics 14:149–65.

Denison, E. 1979. Accounting for Slower Economic Growth. Washington, D.C.: Brookings.

———. 1983. "The Interruption of Productivity Growth in the United States." Economic Journal 93:56–77.

Dery, D. 1984. Problem Definition in Policy Analysis. Lawrence: University of Kansas Press.

Doig, J. W., and E. C. Hargrove, eds. 1988. Leadership and Innovation: A Biographical Perspective on Entrpreneurs in Government. Baltimore: Johns Hopkins University Press.

Donahue, J. D. 1989. The Privatization Decision: Public Ends, Private Means. New York: Basic Books.

Dosi, G., et al., eds. 1988. Technical Change and Economic Theory. London: Pinter.

Downs, G. W. and Larkey, P. D. 1986. The Search for Government Efficiency: From Hubris to Helplessness. Phildadelphia: Temple University Press. Reviews the alternative ways that analysts and policy makers have tried to achieve efficiency. A lighter-hearted look at the government failure literature.

Drell, S., P. J. Farley, and D. Holloway. 1985. *The Reagan Strategic Defense Initiative: A Technical, Political, and Arms Control Assessment.* Boston: Ballinger.

Drzyek, J. 1983. "Don't Toss Coins into Garbage Cans: A Prologue to Policy Design." *Journal of Public Policy* 3:345–68.

Dumas, L. J. 1986. *The Overburdened Economy: Uncovering the Causes of Chronic Unemployment, Inflation, and National Decline.* Berkeley and Los Angeles: University of California Press.

Dupuit, J. 1969. "On the Measurement of the Utility of Public Works." In *Readings in Welfare Economics*, trans. and ed. K. J. Arrow and T. Scitovsky. Homewood, Ill.: Irwin.

Eads, G. C. 1982. "White House Oversight of Executive Branch Regulation." In *Social Regulation: Strategies for Reform*, ed. E. Bardach and R. A. Kagan. New Brunswick, N.J.: Transaction Books.

Eads, G., and R. Nelson. 1971. "Governmental Support for Advanced Civilian Technology: Power Reactors and the Supersonic Transport." *Public Policy* 19:405–27.

Eckstein, O. 1958. *Water Resource Development: the Economics of Project Evaluation.* Cambridge, Mass.: Harvard University Press.

Elkin, S. 1986. "Regulation and Regime: A Comparative Analysis." *Journal of Public Policy* 6:49–72.

Enthoven, A. C., and K. W. Smith. 1971. *Shaping the Defense Program.* New York: Harper and Row.

Federal Inter-Agency River Basin Committee, Subcommittee on Benefits and Costs. 1950. *Report to the Federal Inter-Agency River Basin Committee.* Washington, D.C.: GPO.

Feldman, M. S. 1989. *Order without Design: Information Production and Policy Making.* Stanford, Calif.: Stanford University Press.

Finley, M. I. 1985. *The Ancient Economy.* 2d ed. Berkeley and Los Angeles: University of California Press.

Fischoff, B., S. Lichtenstein, P. Slovic, S. Derby, and R. Keeney. 1984. *Acceptable Risk.* Cambridge: Cambridge University Press.

Freeman, C. 1982. *The Economics of Industrial Innovation.* London: Pinter.

Friedmann, J. 1985. *Planning in the Public Domain: From Knowledge to Action.* Princeton, N.J.: Princeton University Press.

Fromm, G., ed. 1981. *Studies in Public Regulation.* Cambridge, Mass.: MIT Press.

Gansler, J. S. 1986. *The Defense Industry.* Cambridge, Mass.: MIT Press.

Gardner, H. S. 1988. *Comparative Economic Systems.* New York: Dryden Press.

Goldberg, V. 1974. "Institutional Change and the Quasi-Invisible Hand." *Journal of Law and Economics* 17:461–92.

———. 1976. "Regulation and Administered Contracts." *Bell Journal of Economics* 6:426–49.

Goldman, E. F. 1977. *Rendevous with Destiny: A History of Modern American Reform.* New York: Vintage Books.

Golembiewski, R. T., and J. Rabin. eds. 1983. *Public Budgeting and Finance.* 3d ed. New York: Marcel Dekker.

Grabowski, H. 1976. *Drug Regulation and Innovation: Empirical Evidence and Policy Options.* Washington, D.C.: American Enterprise Institute for Public Policy Research.

Grabowski, H., and J. M. Vernon. 1983. *Regulation of Pharmaceuticals: Balancing the Benefits and Risks.* Washington: D.C.: American Enterprise Institute for for Public Policy Research.

Greenberg, D., and P. K. Robins. 1985. "The Changing Role of Social Experiments in Policy Analysis. *Journal of Policy Analysis and Management* 5:340–62.

Greenberger, M. 1983. *Caught Unawares: The Energy Decade in Retrospect.* Cambridge, Mass.: Ballinger. A critical examination of energy modeling and its technical and political deficiencies.

Guerier, S. W., and W. C. Thompson. 1987. *Perspectives on Strategic Defense.* Boulder, Colo.: Westview Press.

Gujarati, D. 1984. *Government and Business.* New York: McGraw-Hill.

Hall, P. 1982. *Great Planning Disasters.* Berkeley and Los Angeles: University of California Press.

Hansman, H. B. 1980. "The Role of Nonprofit Enterprise." *Yale Law Journal* 8:835–91.

Hanusch, H. 1983. *Anatomy of Government Deficiency.* Berlin: Springer-Verlag.

Harberger, A. C. 1954. "Monopoly and Resource Allocation." *American Economic Review* 44:77–87. A seminal article on measuring the social costs of monopoly. Finds that the benefit of eliminating all social loss attributable to monopoly is strikingly low. Generated a dispute that continues to this day.

Hatry, H. 1980. "Pitfalls of Evaluation." In *Pitfalls of Analysis*, ed. G. Majone and E. S. Quade. New York: Wiley.

Hausman, J. A. 1981. "Exact Consumer's Surplus and Deadweight Loss." *American Economic Review* 71:662–76.

Hausman, J. A., and D. Wise, eds. 1985. *Social Experimentation*. Chicago: University of Chicago Press.

Haveman, R. H. 1987. *Poverty Policy and Poverty Research:The Great Society and the Social Sciences*. Madison: University of Wisconsin Press.

———. 1989. "Economics and Public Policy: On the Relevance of Conventional Economic Advice." *Quarterly Review of Economics and Business* 29:6–20.

Hayek, F. 1945. "The Use of Knowledge in Society." *American Economic Review* 35:519–30.

Hayes, R. H., and W. J. Abernathy. 1980. "Managing our Way to Economic Decline." *Harvard Business Review* 58 July August:67–77. A famous critique of American styles of business management, particularly its highly short-run orientation.

Heclo, H. 1977. *A Government of Strangers*. Washington, D.C.: Brookings.

Hill, C. T., and J. M. Utterback. 1979. *Technological Innovation in a Dynamic Economy*. New York: Pergamon Press.

Hillier, G., and G. J. Lieberman. 1980. *Introduction to Operations Research*. Oakland, Calif.: Holden-Day.

Hirschleifer, J. W., and J. G. Riley. 1979. "The Analysis of Uncertainty and Information." *Journal of Economic Literature* 17:1375–1421.

Hirschman, A. O. 1970. *Exit, Voice, and Loyalty*. Cambridge, Mass.: Harvard University Press.

———. 1977. *The Passions and the Interests*. Princeton, N.J.: Princeton University Press.

Hitch, C., and R. McKean. 1960. *The Economics of Defense in the Nuclear Age*. Cambridge, Mass.: Harvard University Press. A classic presentation of economic approaches to allocating resources to defense. Sums up the thrust toward PPBS in the late 1950s and early 1960s. Appears highly optimistic in retrospect on the virtues of program budgeting and searching for efficient trade-offs in the production of public goods. Very good appendix on the mathematics of optimization.

Hodges, R. 1988. *Primitive and Peasant Markets*. New York: Basil Blackwell.

Hogwood, B. W., and L. A. Gunn. 1984. *Policy Analysis for the Real World*. New York: Oxford University Press.

Hogwood, B. W., and G. Peters. 1985. *Pathology of Public Policy*. New York: Oxford University Press.

Horwitch, M. 1982. *Clipped Wings: The American SST Conflict*. Cambridge, Mass.: MIT Press.

Hurwicz, L . 1973. "The Design of Mechanisms for Resource Allocation." *American Economic Review* 63:1–30.

Jackson, P. M. 1983. *The Political Economy of Bureaucracy*. Totowa, N.J.: Barnes and Noble.

Janis, I. 1989. *Crucial Decisions: Leadership in Policymaking and Crisis Management*. New York: Free Press.

Janis, I., and L. Mann. 1977. *Decisionmaking: A Psychological Analysis of Conflict, Choice, and Commitment*. New York: Free Press.

Johnson, C. 1984. *The Industrial Policy Debate*. San Francisco: ICS Press.

Kahn, A. E. 1970. *The Economics of Regulation*. 2 vols. New York: Wiley.

Kamien, M. I., and N. L. Schwartz. 1982. *Market Structure and Innovation*. Cambridge: Cambridge University Press. A good, general survey of the economics of innovation-literature.

Kaufman, H. 1960. *The Forest Ranger*. Baltimore: Johns Hopkins Press.

Keating, B. P., and M. O. Keating. 1980. *Not-for-Profit*. Glen Ridge, N.J.: Horton.

Kelman, S. 1981. *What Price Incentives: Economists and the Environment*. Boston: Auburn House.

———. 1988. *Making Public Policy*. New York: Basic Books.

Kim, J.-C . 1985. "The Market for 'Lemons' Reconsidered: A Model of the Used car Market with Asymmetric Information." *American Economic Review* 75:836–43.

Kirzner, I. 1973. *Competition and Entrepreneurship*. Chicago: University of Chicago Press.

———. 1979. *Perception, Opportunity, and Profit: Studies in the Theory of Entrepreneurship*. Chicago: University of Chicago Press.

Klein, B., and K. B. Leffler. 1981. "The Role of Market Forces in Assuring Contractual Performance." *Journal of Political Economy* 89:615–41.

Klevorick, A. K. 1971. "The Optimal Fair Rate of Return." *Bell Journal of Economics and Management Science* 2:122–53.

Kneese, A. R., and C. Schultze. 1975. *Pollution, Prices, and Public Policy*. Washington, D.C.: Brookings.

Krutilla, J. V. and O. Eckstein. 1958. *Multiple Purpose River Development*. Baltimore: Johns Hopkins University Press.

Laffont, J. 1988. *Fundamentals of Public Economics*. Cambridge, Mass.: MIT Press.

Lauth, T. P. 1978. "Zero-Base Budgeting in Georgia State Government: Myth and Reality." *Public Admininstration Review* 38:420–30.

Lavoie, D. 1985. *National Economic Planning: What Is Left*. Cambridge, Mass.: Ballinger Publishing Company.

Levine, R. A. 1986. *The SDI Debate as a Continuation of History*. Los Angeles: Center for International and Strategic Affairs.

Lewis, E. 1980. *Public Entrepreneurship: Toward a Theory of Bureaucratic Political Power*. Bloomington: Indiana University Press.

Lindblom, C. E., and D. K. Cohen. 1979. *Useable Knowledge*. New Haven, Conn.: Yale University Press.

Loeb, M., and W. A. Magat. 1979. "A Decentralized Method for Utility Regulation." *Journal of Law and Economics* 22:339–404.

Lynch, T. 1985. *Public Budgeting in America*. 2d ed. Englewood Cliffs, N.J.: Prentice-Hall.

Lynch, T., ed. 1981. *Contemporary Public Budgeting*. New Brunswick, N.J.: Transaction Books.

Lynn, L. 1983. *Managing the Public's Business*. New York: Basic Books.

Lyons, G. M. 1969. *The Uneasy Partnership: Social Science and the Federal Government in the Twentieth Century*. New York: Sage.

Maas, A., ed. 1962. *Design of Water Resource Systems*. New York: Macmillan.

McCarthy, T. 1978. *The Critical Theory of Jurgen Habermas*. Cambridge, Mass.: MIT Press.

McCloskey, D. 1983. "The Rhetoric of Economics." *Journal of Economic Literature* 21:481–517. A famous article on method that notes that the actual practice of economics diverges markedly from the positivist ideals economists hold. Observes that positivism as a philosophy is long dead except in economics and that economists use a nonscientific rhetoric in actual policy discussion.

McCraw, T. K., ed. 1981. *Regulation in Perspective: Historical Es-*

says. Cambridge, Mass.: Harvard University Press. A set of interesting essays on the historical development of regulation in the United States. Vogel deals with the history of social regulation in his essay.

McKean, R. 1958. *Efficiency in Government through Systems Analysis*. New York: Wiley. A summative statement of cost-benefit analysis applied to public water projects.

Madaus, G. F., D. L. Stufflebeam, and M. S. Scriven. 1987. "Program Evaluation: A Historical Overview," In *Evaluation Models: Viewpoints on Educational and Human Service Evaluation*, ed. Madaus, Scriven, and Stufflebeam. Boston: Kluwer Nijhoff.

Magat, W. 1976. "Regulation and the Rate and Direction of Induced Technical Change." *Bell Journal of Economics and Management Science* 8:478–95.

Majone, G., and E. Quade, eds. 1980. *Pitfalls of Analysis*. New York: Wiley.

Mansfield, E., A. Romeo, and S. Wagner. 1979. "Social and Private Rates of Return from Industrial Innovations." *Review of Economics and Statistics* 61:49–52.

May, E. R., and R. Neustadt. 1986. *Thinking in Time*. New York: Basic Books. Argues for the use of structured questions or checklists in decision making. Whether this makes for "vigilant" decision making as defined by Janis (1989) is an interesting question.

Meier, K. J. 1985. *Regulation: Politics, Bureaucracy, and Economics*. New York: St. Martin's Press.

Mensch, G. 1979. *The Technological Stalemate*. Cambridge, Mass.: Ballinger.

Mikesell, J. L. 1986. *Fiscal Administration*. Chicago: Dorsey Press.

Miller, G. J., and T. M. Moe. 1983. "Bureaucrats, Legislators, and the Size of Government." *American Political Science Review* 77:297–322.

Mills, E. S., and P. E. Graves. 1986. *The Economics of Environmental Quality*. New York: Norton.

Mishan, E. J. 1980. *Introduction to Normative Economics*. New York: Oxford University Press.

———. 1982a. *Cost-Benefit Analysis*. New York: Allen and Unwin.

———. 1982b. *What Political Economy Is All About*. Cambridge: Cambridge University Press

Mitnick, B. M. 1980. *The Political Economy of Regulation*. New York: Columbia University Press. One of the very few works to address regulatory problems and agencies from their birth to their death.

Mockyr, J., ed. 1985. *The Economics of the Industrial Revolution.* Totowa, N.J.: Rowman and Allanheld.

Morey, E. R. 1984. "Confuser Surplus." *American Economic Review* 74:163—73.

Morris, P.W.G., and G. H. Hough. 1987. *The Anatomy of Major Projects: A Study of the Reality of Project Management.* New York: Wiley.

Mosher, F. C. 1979. *A Tale of Two Agencies: A Comparative Analysis of the General Accounting Office and the Office of Management and Budget.* Baton Rouge: Louisiana State University Press.

Moulin, H. 1983. *The Strategy of Social Choice.* New York: North Holland.

Murnane, R. J., and R. R. Nelson. 1984. "Production and Innovation When Techniques Are Tacit." *Journal of Economic Behavior and Organization,* 5:353–73. A good discussion of the difference between "hard," well-defined technologies presumably available to firms and the "soft" ones used by bureaucracies.

Murphy, F. H., and A. L. Soyster. 1982. "Optimal Output of the Averch-Johnson Model." *Atlantic Economic Journal* 10:77–81.

National Science Board. 1988. *Science and Engineering Indicators—1989.* Washington, D.C.: GPO.

Needham, D. 1983. *The Economics and Politics of Regulation: A Behavioral Approach.* Boston: Little, Brown.

Nelkin, D. 1971. *The Politics of Housing Innovation.* Ithaca, N.Y.: Cornell University Press.

Nelson, R. R. 1959. "The Simple Economics of Basic Research." *Journal of Political Economy* 12:193–211.

———. 1981. "Assessing Private Enterprise: An Exegesis of Tangled Doctrine." *Bell Journal of Economics and Management Science* 12:93–111.

———. 1984. *High Technology Policies: A Five Nation Comparison.* Washington, D.C.: American Enterprise Research for Public Policy Research.

Nelson, R. R., and S. G. Winter. 1982. *An Evolutionary Theory of Economic Change.* Cambridge, Mass.: Harvard University Press. An excellent overview and critique of the neoclassical theory of the firm. Nelson's and Winter's work, however, shows how difficult it is to obtain analytic results of interest

to economists once one departs from neoclasical theory. Re-
sorts to simulation to illustrate its "theory." Simulations show
that evolutionary theory can explain data as well as neoclassical theory, but simulations can be "tuned" to show what ever
the investigator desires.

Neuberger, E., and W. J. Duffy. 1976. *Comparative Economic Systems: A Decision-Making Approach*. Boston: Allyn and Bacon.

Niskanen, W. 1971. *Bureaucracy and Representative Government*.
Chicago: Aldine-Atherton.

North, D. C. 1981. *Structure and Change in Economic History*. New
York: Norton.

North, D. C., and Thomas, R. P. 1973. *The Rise of the Western World*.
New York: Norton. The North-Thomas transactions cost view
can be fruitfully compared with the Rosenberg-Birdzell
technological-legal view of the rise of the West.

Novick, D., ed. 1965. *Program Budgeting: Program Analysis and the
Federal Budget*. Cambridge, Mass.: Harvard University Press.
Very clear exposition of program budgeting concepts and requirements written by well-known champions of the technique. Written at the high-water mark of belief in the effectiveness of program budgeting, just at the time President Johnson
extended PPBS to the entire federal government. Economists'
strong belief that PPBS would make federal resource allocation problems much more rational is affecting almost twenty-
five years later.

O'Connell, J. F. 1982. *Welfare Economic Theory*. Boston: Auburn
House.

Office of Science and Technology Policy. 1982. *Annual Science and
Technology Report to the Congress: 1982*. Washington, D.C.:
Office of Science and Technology Policy.

Office of Technology Assessment. 1988. *SDI: Technology, Surviv-
ability, and Software*. Washington, D.C.: Office of Technology
Assessment.

Olson, M. 1965. *The Logic of Collective Action*. Cambridge, Mass.:
Harvard University Press.

——. 1982. *The Rise and Decline of Nations*. New Haven, Conn:
Yale University Press.

Ozaki, R. S. 1984. "How Japanese Industrial Policy Works." In *The
Industrial Development Debate*, ed. C. Johnson. San Francisco: ICS Press.

Pack, J. R. 1989. "Privatization and Cost Reduction." *Policy Science*
22:1–25.

208 References

Patton, C. V., and D. S. Sawicki. 1986. *Basic Methods of Policy Analysis and Planning*. Englewood Cliffs, N.J.: Prentice-Hall.

Pearce, D. W. 1983. *Cost-Benefit Analysis*. 2d ed. New York: St. Martin's Press.

Pearce, D. W., and A. K. Dasgupta. 1972. *Cost-Benefit Analysis: Theory and Practice*. New York: Barnes and Noble.

Peck, J., and F. Scherer. 1962. *The Weapons Acquisition Process: An Economic Analysis*. Boston: Harvard University Graduate School of Business Administration.

Pejhovic, S. 1983. *Philosophical and Economic Foundations of Capitalism*. Lexington, Mass.: Lexington Books.

Peltzman, S. 1976. "Toward a More General Theory of Regulation." *Journal of Law and Economics* 19:211–40.

———. 1989. "The Economic Theory of Regulation after a Decade of Deregulation." In *Brookings Papers on Economic Activity: Microeconomics*, ed. M. N. Baily and C. Winston. Washington, D.C.: Brookings.

Perrow, C. 1986. *Complex Organizations: A Critical Essay*. 3d ed. New York: Random House.

Petersen, H. C. 1985. *Business and Government*. 2d ed. New York: Harper & Row.

Phlips, P. 1988. *The Economics of Imperfect Information*. Cambridge: Cambridge University Press.

Phyrr, P. A. 1973. *Zero-Based Budgeting*. New York: Wiley.

Pierce, W. S. 1981. *Bureaucratic Failure and Public Expenditure*. New York: Academic Press. An early and acute entry in the literature of government failure. Constructs a large number of propositions about failure and then tests them with case studies.

Posner, R. A. 1970. "A Statistical Study of Antitrust Enforcement." *Journal of Law and Economics* 13:365–419.

———. "The Social Cost of Monopoly and Regulation." *Journal of Political Economy* 83:807–27.

Presidential Commission on the Accident at Three Mile Island. 1979. *Report of the President's Commission on the Accident at Three Mile Island*. Washington, D.C.: GPO.

Presidential Commission on the Space Shuttle Challenger Disaster. 1986. *Report to the President*. Washington, D.C.: GPO.

Quade, E., and H. Miser, eds. 1985. *Handbook of Systems Analysis: Overview of Uses, Procedures, and Applications*. New York: Elsevier.

Quirk, J., and R. Saposnick. 1968. *Introduction to General Equilibrium Theory and Welfare Economics*. New York: McGraw-Hill.

Rawls, J. 1971. *A Theory of Justice*. Cambridge, Mass.: Harvard University Press.

Ray, A. 1984. *Cost-Benefit Analysis: Issues and Methodologies*. Baltimore: Johns Hopkins University Press.

Rees, R. 1984. *Public Enterprise Economics*. 2d ed. New York: St. Martin's Press.

Rhoads, S. 1985. *The Economist's View of the World: Government, Markets, and Public Policy*. Cambridge: Cambridge University Press.

Rivlin, A. 1971. *Systematic Thinking for Social Action*. Washington, D.C.: Brookings. Represents the high-water mark of optimism about the power of social science research to reveal correct public policy.

Rosen, S. 1987. "Systems Analysis and the Quest for Rational Defense." In *Policy Studies: Review Annual*, vol. 8, ed. R. C. Rist. New Brunswick, N.J.: Transaction Books.

Rosenberg, N. 1982. *Inside the Black Box: Technology and Economics*. Cambridge: Cambridge University Press.

Rosenberg, N., and L. E. Birdzell, Jr. 1986. *How the West Got Rich*. New York: Basic Books.

Rossi, P. H., and H. E. Freeman. 1982. *Evaluation: A Systematic Approach*. 2d ed. Beverly Hills, Calif.: Sage Publications. A good textbook on techniques and designs for doing evaluation.

Rothenberg, J. 1975. "Cost-Benefit Analysis: A Methodological Exposition." In *Handbook of Evaluation Research*, vol. 2, ed. E. Shrenig and M. Guttentag. Beverly Hills, Calif.: Sage Publications.

Sapolsky, H. 1972. *The Polaris Missile System: Bureaucratic and Programmatic Success in Government*. Cambridge, Mass.: Harvard University Press.

Savas, E. S. 1987. *Privatization: The Key to Better Government*. Chatham, N.J.: Chatham House.

Sayles, L., and M. Chandler. 1971. *Managing Large Scale Systems*. New York: Harper & Row.

Schelling, T. C., ed. 1983. *Incentives for Environmental Control*. Cambridge, Mass.: MIT Press.

Schick, A. 1973. "A Death in the Bureaucracy." *Public Administration Review* 33:146–50.

Schotter, A. 1985. *Free Market Economics*. New York: St. Martin's Press. An interesting elementary text that explains why market systems inevitably contain elements of market failure.

Schulman, P. R. 1975. "Nonincremental Policy Making: Notes Toward an Alternative Paradigm." *American Political Science Review* 69:1354–70.

———. 1980. *Large Scale Decisionmaking*. New York: Greenwood Press.

Schultze, C. 1977. *The Public Use Of Private Interest*. Washington, D.C.: Brookings. Well-reasoned arguments for the possible superiority of market mechanisms over centrally directed ones from a prominent economist and policy practitioner.

Schumpeter, J. 1947. *Capitalism, Socialism, and Democracy*. 2d ed. New York: Harper and Row.

Selznick, P. 1949. *TVA and the Grass Roots*. Berkeley and Los Angeles: University of California Press.

Sharkey, W. 1982. *The Theory of Natural Monopoly*. Cambridge: Cambridge University Press.

Shepherd, W. G. 1984. "Contestability vs. Competition." *American Economic Review* 74:572–87.

Shepsle, K. A. 1984. "Political Solutions to Market Problems." *American Political Science Review* 78:417–34. One of the few articles that directly compare market solutions to allocation problems to legislative solutions. Assuming legislators have objective functions that are purely local in their arguments, the analysis shows that there is a divergence between optimal market solutions and optimal political solutions.

Sieber, S. 1981. *Fatal Remedies: The Ironies of Social Intervention*. New York: Plenum Press. Sieber argues that many social interventions work in an unintended manner to make the situations they are supposed to cure worse. Some programs are not only inefficient and ineffective, but also truly counterproductive in their consequences. In addition to Sieber, Hall (1982), Hogwood and Peters (1985), Pierce (1981), and Wolf (1979, 1988) provide a good introduction to nonmarket or government failure.

Simon, H. 1965. *Administrative Behavior: A Study of Decisionmaking Processes*. 2d ed. New York: Free Press.

Spulber, D. F. 1989. *Regulation and Markets*. Cambridge, Mass.: MIT Press.

Stigler, G. S. 1971. "The Economic Theory of Regulation." *Bell Journal of Economics and Management Science* 2:3–21.

Stiglitz, J. E. 1986. "Theory of Competition, Incentives, and Risk." In *New Developments in the Analysis of Market Structure*, ed. J. E. Stiglitz and G. F. Mathewson. Cambridge, Mass.: MIT Press.

———. 1988. *Economics of the Public Sector*. 2d ed. New York: Norton.

Stockman, D. 1986. *The Art of Politics*. New York: Harper and Row. Stockman's account of his tenure as President Reagan's first OMB director is obviously biased, but he does capture the dealings and deal making characteristic of high-level debate over the direction of the political economy.

Stokey, E., and R. Zeckhauser. 1978. *A Primer for Policy Analysis*. New York: Norton.

Stoneman, P. 1983. *The Economic Analysis of Technological Change*. New York: Oxford University Press.

Stubbing, R. A. 1986. *The Defense Game*. New York: Harper & Row.

Sugden, R. 1981. *The Political Economy of Public Choice*. New York: Halsted Press.

Sylvia, R. D., K. J. Meier, and E. M. Gunn. 1985. *Program Planning and Evaluation for the Public Manager*. Monterey, Calif.: Brooks/Cole Publishing.

Taylor, S. 1984. *Making Bureaucracies Think: The Environmental Impact Strategy of Administrative Reform*. Stanford, Calif.: Stanford University Press.

Thompson, M. S. 1980. *Benefit-Cost Analysis for Program Evaluation*. Beverly Hills, Calif.: Sage Publications.

Titmuss, R. M. 1971. *The Gift Relationship: From Human Blood to Social Policy*. New York: Pantheon Books.

Trebing, H. M. 1984. "Public Utility Regulation: A Case Study in the Debate of Effectiveness of Economic Regulation. *Journal of Economic Issues* 18:223–50.

Tribe, L. H. 1973. "Technology Assessment and the Fourth Dimension: The Limits of Instrumental Rationality." *Southern California Law Review* 46:617–60.

Tullock, G. 1965. *The Politics of Bureaucracy*. Washington, D.C.: Public Affairs Press.

Union of Concerned Scientists. 1984. *The Fallacy of Star Wars*. New York: Vintage Books.

Usher, D. 1964. "The Welfare Economics of Innovation." *Economica* 31:279–87.

———. 1981. *The Economic Prerequisite to Democracy*. New York: Columbia University Press.

Vickers, G. 1983. *The Art of Judgment*. New York: Harper & Row. Vickers presents probably the best written explanation of what it takes to make judgments and decisions in the public domain.

Ward, B. 1979. *The Ideal Worlds of Economics*. New York: Random House.

Weimer, D. L., and V. R. Aidan. 1989. *Policy Analysis: Concepts and Practice*. Englewood Cliffs, N. J.: Prentice-Hall.

Weintraub, E. R. 1985. *General Equilibrium Analysis: Studies in Appraisal*. Cambridge: Cambridge University Press.

Weiss, L. W., and M. Klass, eds. 1981. *Case Studies in Regulation and Reform*. Boston: Little, Brown.

Weiss, L. W., and M. Klass, eds. 1986. *Regulatory Reform: What Actually Happened*. Boston: Little, Brown.

Westfield, F. M. 1970. "Innovation and Monopoly Regulation." In *Technological Change in Regulated Industries*, ed. W. M. Capron. Washington, D.C.: Brookings.

Wholey, J. S., M. A. Abramson, and C. Bellavita, eds. 1986. *Performance and Credibility: Developing Excellence in Public and Nonprofit Organizations*. Lexington, Mass.: Lexington Books. Argues that improved performance in public and nonprofit organizations can be achieved by the judicious application of the evaluator's art. Presents some cases purporting to show this, but does not present any evaluation failures.

Wildavsky, A. 1966. "The Political Economy of Efficiency: Cost-Benefit Analysis, System Analysis, and Program Budgeting." *Public Administration Review* 26:292–310.

———. 1979. *The Politics of the Budgetary Process*. 3d ed. Boston: Little, Brown.

———. 1988. *The New Politics of the Budgetary Process*. Glenview, Ill.: Scott, Foresman. An update of Wildavsky (1979) that reflects recent changes in federal budgeting. Finds that budgeting has become less marginalist than it used to be because of fundamental disagreements over the purposes of federal spending.

Williamson, O. E. 1985. *The Economic Institutions of Capitalism*. New York: Free Press. An explanation and summary of the author's work on the transactions cost approach to economics and economic theory.

Willig, R. 1976. "Consumer's Surplus Without Apology." *American Economic Review* 66:589–97.

Wilson, J. Q. 1989. *Bureaucracy: What Government Agencies Do and Why They Do It*. New York: Basic Books.

Wittman, D. 1989. "Why Democracies Produce Efficient Results." *Journal of Political Economy* 97:1395–1424.

Wolf, C., Jr. 1969. "The Present Value of the Past." Rand Corporation, P-4067. Unpublished.

———. 1979. "The Theory of Nonmarket Failure: Framework for Implementation Analysis." *Journal of Law and Economics* 22:107–39.

———. 1988. *Markets and Government: Choosing between Imperfect Alternatives*. Cambridge, Mass.: MIT Press.

Wolff, E. N. 1987. *Growth, Accumulation, and Unproductive Activity: An Analysis of the Postwar U.S. Economy*. Cambridge: Cambridge University Press.

Wonnacott, R. J., and T. H. Wonnacott. 1979. *Econometrics*. 2d ed. New York: Wiley.

Woolridge, R. J., ed. 1981. *Evaluation of Complex Systems*. Washington, D.C.: Jossey-Bass.

Worthley, J. A., and W. G. Ludwin. 1979. *Zero-Base Budgeting in State and Local Government: Current Experiences and Cases*. New York: Praeger.

Index

Acceptability: as criterion for evaluating strategy, 8, 23, 118

Allocation strategies, appraisal of, 7, 9, 172, 176n2; design of criteria for, 8–9; of economic systems, 175n1; weighting criteria in, 9–10

Allocative efficiency, 52, 91, 108, 115

Allocative ineffiency, 34, 187n18

Bargaining, in markets; 27; in planning and budgeting, 113, 132; over appropriate allocation stragegy, 69, 102, 123, 132

BCA. *See* Benefit-cost analysis

Bendor, J., 71

Benefit-cost analysis (BCA): and aggregate willingness to pay, 139–42; appraisal of, 159–61; criticism of, 192n8; defined strictly, 189n3; and discount rates, 143–45; history of, 135–37; and information, 148; logic of, 134, 137–39; and operations research (OR), 136–37; and problems in estimating costs, 142–43;

and rules of thumb and decision making, 145–49; and technical barriers to use of, 140–42; and tests of utility, 146–48; theory of, 134, 137–38; versus learning by doing, 158–59

Budgeting, critical assumptions about, 124–25; and potential for strategic behavior, 125

Budget maximization models for bureaus, 58–62, 66–71

Budgets, of bureaus: evaluation and reform of, 126–27; incremental increases in, 71–72; and ideology, 130; and information, 126; maximization of, 58–62, 66–71; as measure of performance, 81–82; as measure of power and success, 56; and output, 63–69; output-oriented, hazards of, 125–27; and pressure to spend, 83–84; and sunk costs, 85–86

Budgets and planning: appraisal of systems for, 131–33

Bureaus: allocative and technical inefficiency of, 60; and BCA: 135–49; and budget

Pitt Series in Policy and Institutional Studies
Bert A. Rockman, Editor